The
SIKH
in the Snow

MY TRAVEL CONFESSIONS

The SIKH in the Snow

MY TRAVEL CONFESSIONS

Inder Raj Ahluwalia

STERLING

STERLING PAPERBACKS
An imprint of
Sterling Publishers (P) Ltd.
Regd. Office: A-59, Okhla Industrial Area, Phase-II,
New Delhi-110020. CIN: U22110PB1964PTC002569
Tel: 26387070, 26386209
E-mail: mail@sterlingpublishers.in
www.sterlingpublishers.in

The Sikh in the Snow
© 2019, Inder Raj Ahluwalia
ISBN 978 93 86245 51 9

All rights are reserved.
No part of this publication may be reproduced, stored in a retrieval system or transmitted, in any form or by any means, mechanical, photocopying, recording or otherwise, without prior written permission of the author.

Printed in India
Printed and Published by Sterling Publishers Pvt. Ltd., New Delhi-110020.

Contents

	My Life Thus Far	7
1.	The Sikh in the Snow	10
2.	The Red Carpet	19
3.	Malaysia, Truly Nostalgia	30
4.	Auckland, Actually	39
5.	An Omani Interlude	46
6.	Seven Days in Singapore	63
7.	Jewels in the Forest	72
8.	Two Days in Chitwan	84
9.	Gstaad Gasps	89
10.	Khantoke and Softness	93
11.	The Turbaned Groom	98
12.	The Hague	104
13.	A Dance on the Elbe	108
14.	Guinness: Good Health	114
15.	Marche, Maybe	118

16.	Glacially Exotic	125
17.	A Tale of One City	133
18.	Biking Girls and a Brilliant Talk	141
19.	Shalom	150
20.	Bushmen and Jungle Skills	157
21.	A Bow in Downtown Tokyo	164
22.	Frolicking by the Fjords	174
23.	Santa Bhai	182
24.	Spa Sparring	189
25.	No. 7	198
26.	"Kuch Kuch" Kaohsiung	207
27.	Quantum of Solace	212
28.	The Blessings Seeker	221

My Life Thus Far

My life has been a roller-coaster ride, and I suppose it makes an interesting story.

Ever since I started writing about my travels way back in 1980, my story has been one of living here, there and everywhere for long periods while travelling abroad, finally coming home to Delhi, before going off again.

When I first embarked on travel-writing, I honestly didn't know that this would become my career for life, in fact my life itself – my very reason for being!

But that's what happened. The writing became easy, the travels were joyous, and I made friends with people across the globe. I met thousands of people across the fifty-odd countries I visited – some several times – and found an abundance of kindness, friendship and love. And a little bit of romance, too, I must confess.

Now that I've brought up this business of romance, let me tackle it straightaway and get it out of the way without further ado.

Thanks to my being a travel journalist and world-traveller, and thanks to my being single, some women consider me exotic. My profession gives an exotic, envious touch to my isolation and gives me the mystery man aura.

While women in general consider me enigmatic, some of them feel uneasy when I'm around. They fidget uneasily if I enlighten their husbands about exotic lands. Or about beach holidays, wildlife safaris, mountain trekking, dune-bashing in the desert. It's all quite needless and unnecessary really, and most disconcerting, these women seem to think. So much for that!

I've had the pleasure of visiting stunningly beautiful places that have still managed to remain secrets – regions of immense beauty enhanced by geographical diversity, historical legacies, cultural richness and the distinct lifestyles of their inhabitants. These are the unforgettable vistas of nature that include deep oceans, endless beaches, the world's oldest desert, wildlife, safaris that bond one with nature, blazing sunsets that create the right setting for romance; leisurely cruises that take guests in hand and spoil them thoroughly; cuisines that incorporate not just the food but also local heritage and traditions; and people who showcase their culture to the hilt, and seem to enjoy themselves while doing it.

I'm talking about the world's mightiest fjords; of the Arctic region's pristine beauty; and of wooded mountains shrouded in mist.

But while my life has been supremely adventurous and immensely interesting, it has been at an enormous price tag. It has been a life spent somewhat contrary to accepted norms – career, marriage, children, stability. A life spent chasing rainbows. A life spent mainly pursuing my passion for writing and travelling. A life spent watching people and the world go by from the outside. A life spent marking time rather pleasantly in a beautiful, magical crystal palace.

I know there's so much I haven't done and seen. And probably never will. But it's what I have done and seen that

I feel I must share, simply because it is rare, special, and intensely beautiful. This is my way of sharing it all with all those who are interested to learn how mysterious and beautiful the world really is.

I guess I'll just keep going on till I can. Stay with me! At the risk of sounding vain let me say that it isn't every day in your life that you'll get to see a Sikh in the snow.

1

The Sikh in the Snow

The sign proclaimed it was 11 degrees below zero outside. But even then outside was where everyone wanted to be. Thirty minutes on the highway can get into your head on the Tyrolean Alps. Especially with the snow coming down in sheets, shrouding everything.

Innsbruck behind me, I'd driven gingerly along through snowy, mountain-rimmed meadows to end up in the town's centre, knee-deep in snow but basking in sunshine.

They advertise Seefeld as a town where "one won't need palm trees, sand and sea, the only sea on offer being the 'See' in the name Seefeld". Well, fair enough. Everyone's entitled to their vanity.

It doesn't take long to realize that the place is quite special. Unmatched in its opportunities for pleasurable holidays, the Tyrolean mountain region is an outdoors person's paradise, offering unlimited possibilities for winter sports. Quite fittingly, the town was chosen twice as the venue for Winter Olympic Games.

Located at the gate to the Karwendel Preserve, Europe's largest unpopulated mountain area, at 1,200 metres Seefeld is made for outdoor activities. There are lush meadows and forests for those inclined to observe nature's beauty and plenty for exercise and adventure seekers. There are 100 km of nature walks and solitary trails of all grades of difficulty for recreational and more demanding hikes; vertical and extreme rock faces for the climbers among the mountaineers; and rafting in the raging forces of Tyrolean waters in acclaimed runs that take you through spectacular scenery.

It's wise to limber up. You can run up climbing-paths with safety devices, stop at mountain cabins for refreshments, follow marked hiking-paths at high altitudes, take guided hikes and above all, enjoy the unique scenery.

In their bid to make Seefeld a popular family destination, local authorities have created plenty of activities for the young. The Olympia indoor swimming pool has separate pools for children, besides skateboards, in-line skates and mountain bikes. The message is clear. They want kids to visit, too.

As with many of the world's famous sites, it was only a matter of time before golfers discovered and exploited the region's unique natural charms. And with good reason. You get to play on Alpine pastures in fresh air on an 18-hole championship course, surrounded by forests and mountains, the only sound being cow-bells chiming in the distance. The game's popularity in these paradise-like surroundings led to the establishment of the Golf Academy, which offers ideal training grounds in the very heart of Seefeld.

For those who prefer larger balls and a racket, there's "total tennis" at the famous Swedish tennis school which helped players like Borg, Edberg and Wilander become the game's icons.

My town discovery trip was short and sweet. Braving an icy wind, I trudged through the snow to the charming little square with trendy boutiques and lively bistros that passes off as the town centre. Here you do the traditional coffee-and-cakes stop. Tourists thronged the square, outnumbering the few enterprising locals who were up and about, giving a busy look to the area.

As I was moving around, I noticed a young couple had sort of joined me. We nodded and smiled at one another, and went about our tour with serious intent.

A fist-time visitor should also stop by at the beautiful little Gothic church in the centre of town and also at the small Seekirchl church. You can also imbibe a bit of local culture by taking a guided tour of the art exhibitions on biology and natural history.

As in most of Austria, culture and tradition plays a major role in the local lifestyle. For such a small place, there's plenty happening throughout the year. There are merry get-togethers with church concerts, brass-band concerts, comic peasant-plays and folk-music evenings. There's a summer flower festival, a flower parade in August and a winter snow festival.

The day had quickly slipped by and when it was time for dinner, my two friends—Alex and Olga —asked me if I'd care to join them. I was happy to agree and some fifteen minutes later we were seated at a popular local establishment. Dinner was in soft light, over a popular folk dance that depicted the ritual of wooing and proposing, the boys looking suitably bashful, the girls looking suitably maidenly.

Seefeld by night —well, it is a small resort-town, remember. The nightlife's somewhat subdued, but there's enough to keep you in good spirits. Riding on the copious entertainment bandwagon are romantic wine cellars and cosy evenings with music being played on the zither, cool pubs and hot discos and some quality restaurants. There's wine tasting for connoisseurs, performances of international stars and night taxis for the night owls.

Dinner done, we paid up and were saying our goodbyes when Olga casually asked me if I travelled a lot to very cold places. On my replying that I did, she said she'd kind of guessed it because I looked rather comfortable in the snow.

Well, it wasn't something I'd ever been credited for earlier in my life and I didn't quite know what to make of it, so I decided to take it as a compliment. As we moved on together, I felt comforted that I wasn't left out in the cold.

Shortly after this trip, I found myself amid snow once again and this time it was in that very special place on this planet that is reached by crossing the Arctic Circle.

The Arctic region is nothing short of spectacular. I've been fortunate enough to visit several times and each trip brought its share of excitement, thrills and romance. In fact, an abundant of all!

Deep inside the Arctic Circle, situated on the shores of the Torne River, in the old village of Jukkasjarvi in Swedish Lapland, the Ice Hotel is the world's largest igloo, opening its freezing doors to welcome guests from all over the world to wonder at its extraordinariness and beauty, enjoy its cool environs and hospitality and admire the midnight sun and the spectacular Northern Lights (aurora borealis).

Auroras are a unique natural phenomenon that occur around the earth's north and south geomagnetic poles in regions known as auroral ovals. Southern auroras are called aurora australis and northern ones, aurora borealis. They occur because the earth's magnetic field interacts with the solar winds, a tenuous mix of charged particles blowing away the sun.

Somewhat similar to light from colour television, auroral lights result from the air glowing, as charged particles, particularly electrons, rain along the earth's magnetic field lines. The colour of the aurora depends on the type of atom or molecule struck by the charged particles.

Auroral displays vary from night to night and even during a single night. Usually, if sun-earth conditions produce auroral sub-storm, a diffuse patch of glowing sky will be seen first, followed by a discrete arc that brightens, perhaps a thousand-fold, in a minute.

Appearing within the arcs are upward reaching striations aligned with the magnetic field, giving the impression of curtains of light. Ripples and curls dance along the arc curtains and pulsating patches of light may appear in the morning hours.

So much for the Northern Lights.

On my first visit, the Ice Hotel took me completely by surprise. Not just because of its spectacular features, of which there are many, but also because of its guest list that comprised eminent personalities from around the world.

More by accident than design, within an hour of checking-in at the hotel, I found myself seated in the Absolut Ice Bar, an institution by itself, made up entirely of ice and snow, like the entire hotel itself. All hotel bars become logical rendezvous points for the establishment's guests, but none more so than this one.

This is where guests gather for drinks and gossip. Naturally, vodka is the favoured drink, with straight vodka copiously quaffed from tumblers made of ice. That this is a happening place is obvious from the guests' profile. Chances are you may be rubbing shoulders with the Swedish Royal couple or the Irish President. Or perhaps with models Naomi Campbell or Kate Moss, or the Swedish model Marcus Schenkenberg. Or famous photographer Herb Ritts. Or Swedish rock star Jennifer Brown. Or the American rock band Van Halen. You name the world celebrities and chances are they have been here.

Getting into the spirit of things, I warmed up with an Absolut Blue, a mix of Absolut vodka and blueberry syrup. You can lean over the huge bar table of solid ice, perch on ice stools, or just relax in the seating area with its ice chairs and tables, complete with ashtrays. The glasses are carved from ice and the alcohol stored in special cold-resistant bottles. Once used, the glasses are just heaped into a corner to form a block that stays there till the entire hotel melts down.

Clutching my ice glass in my gloved hand, I sipped my drink and looked around to see if there was anyone around with whom I could strike up a conversation and possibly a friendship.

To my surprise, and enormous delight, I *did* meet someone interesting. And a very pretty lady she was, too. Her name was Suki and she was travelling around Scandinavia, escorting a group of tourists.

While I'd been busy examining the texture and flavour of my drink, Suki had walked into the bar and seated herself not too far away from me. When our eyes met, we nodded and smiled at each other and then, as if it had triggered some sort of a signal, she came up to me and introduced herself. It was simply wonderful.

We made the usual small-talk and Suki appeared comfortable and relaxed, which in turn made me feel the same also.

On the spur of the moment, I asked her if she's like to do a sort of tour and discover the hotel. "Oh, how gallant of you to offer to accompany me and show me around," she said with a smile.

"Some special things are reserved for special people," I said."And for you, a conducted tour with a personal escort." I tried my own version of a smile. "Sounds good. As a tour leader I do nothing but show people around. It will be nice to be escorted for once, and that too by a turbaned travel journalist," she replied warmly.

We said goodbye to the bartenders, did our bit by heaping a few glasses on to the pile in the corner and left the freezing watering hole.

We walked along a corridor, shoulder to shoulder and gradually the circulation in my legs came back and they stopped feeling like jelly. We poked our heads into a couple of empty rooms, then worked our way through another corridor into the huge colonnaded halls and public exhibition galleries. We stopped to admire the carving and sculpture exhibits on display, the way travelling couples with time to kill do in museums and art galleries. We then moved on to the cinema, where the projector is stored in a refrigerator. Light filtered through the ice walls, casting ghostly shadows on everything, creating an alabaster effect. Like beacons in the mist, little lamps flickered gently, each marking its territory. It was all quiet, serene and immensely beautiful.

Outside, the snow fell gently, shrouding the ice sculptures in the garden. Inside, the exhibits shone brightly. It was pure magic.

The last stop of our so-called conducted tour was the chapel. I literally lured Suki there. Why? I don't know. Maybe because it was so beautiful, maybe because she was so beautiful, or maybe because by now I'd realized I needed divine help.

Whatever may be the case, the fact is that the chapel was exquisite. You can pray amid an ice altar, ice benches, pews and gospel carvings. I could see that Suki was deeply moved by the place. Everyone is. The temperature may have dropped, but I was warming up.

I told her that the hotel arranges marriages and christenings, subject to one condition. Babies must have the word "is" (Swedish for ice) in their names. So all those with names like Christopher, Isak, Doris or Isabella, can get easily christened in the only ice-chapel in the world. "And if your name does have the word 'is' in it and you aren't married, well, I'll tell you how to go about it," I added in a loud whisper, thoroughly pleased with myself for being so clever.

She gave me a long, questioning sort of look and smiled.

It had been snowing lightly but steadily for the past couple of hours, and the landscape had acquired a look that only fresh, driven snow can give. It was a world of white. Airy, white crystals of snowflakes filled up the canvas of our vision, shrouding everything. They landed softly on her head, bounced off her forehead and fell softly to the ground. A few managed to entangle themselves in my beard.

A thought flashed through my mind. Across the Arctic Circle, in arguably the last frontier of European wilderness, under the phantom glow of the Northern Lights, I was sitting with one of the most beautiful woman I had ever met.

"You know, there's a strong possibility that we'll never meet again," she said in a soft tone. I wanted to say something appropriate, but was so deflated by what she'd just said that no words came to me. To my surprise, the silence seemed to go down well with her. We sat for a while and then she got up and gave me a hug. And left. Just like that. One moment she was there, and the next she was gone. She just faded away and disappeared in the snow.

Morning brought sunshine and a balmy minus seven degrees temperature. Suki was gone. She'd checked out with her group at the crack of dawn and had left a note for me.

"Thank you for the magical moments. And for your understanding. Maybe I hadn't realized it, but I think I needed to meet and spend some time with someone like you. You calmed me and made me pick myself up. I'll never forget the time we spent together. I particularly appreciate the way you responded. You're a gallant man. Or should I say, you're a gallant Sikh in the snow."

2

The Red Carpet

I walked the red carpet! And that says it all, really.

But first, I walked from the Carlton to the Palais des Festivals, and as things transpired, that became a story in itself. Let me tell you a little bit about Cannes, first.

Cannes is a town that lives up to all the hype built around it. It's got the glitz, the glamour, and the pizzazz. It's got what I call a glamour buzz. People are right when they say the town is the stuff of dreams and legends. And that is precisely what has made it such a centre of glamour and over the years spawned so many stories of so many celebrities and their famous lifestyles.

Come its annual film festival time, and things get rather exciting. It is almost as if there is a Cannes within Cannes. Everything becomes sort of larger than life. It's all a bit special and rather heady because of the glamour and opulence on display.

I had been visiting the city for some twenty years, but this was the very first occasion when I had arrived at film festival time. If, as they say, there's no business-like show business, let me tell you there's no place like the French Riviera, no city quite like Cannes, especially during its annual film festival, and no hotel quite like the legendary Carlton which has played host to world leaders and film stars for several decades now.

During this period, Carlton isn't just your normal, super-deluxe hotel. It's a big blur of opulence and glamour that everyone dreams about. So if you've made it here at this particular time, you've obviously done something in your life to earn it. Well, that's what I told myself anyway. And believe me, it felt good!

All my other faults notwithstanding, I know for sure I'm not a snob. So this one is a one-off for me. At the risk of sounding profanely vain, I saw there was a clear demarcation in visitor profiles. There were the "us", the lucky ones going to see the movies. And there were the "them", the ordinary folk who happened to be in town in their thousands that balmy summer evening.

My adventure started at the Carlton Hotel itself, where I'd been fortunate enough to stay while attending the 62nd Cannes Film Festival.

I'd arrived at around noon, checked in, and was ready for action. Things were rather well, with a truly grand lunch at the Carlton Beach with Narjiss, the hotel's director.

A Carlton Beach lunch is a tradition and reserved for the privileged. Sitting across the table from Narjiss was and experience by itself. It was stupendous. She looked stunningly beautiful, tall, statuesque, and seemed to glide rather than walk. If I hadn't known her from earlier, I would be forgiven for mistaking her for a Hollywood superstar, which were plenty around.

Being a director in the town's most famous hotel, and especially during the film festival, means a busy time, to say the least. But Narjiss was gracious enough to say she had all the time in the world for me. By that time my head was pounding more than the Mediterranean Sea just ten metres from where we sat with the varied delights of the celebrated Carlton kitchen in front of us.

It was one of those moments in life – I didn't want the lunch to end, but it finally did. An hour and two cups of strong coffee later, I caught up with my friends Gisele and Jean Paul Falot, who'd driven down from their home a hundred kilometres away, to see me, their friend, "the man who stayed at the Carlton". While I was greeting them with a sense of modesty I didn't really feel, Narjiss appeared out of nowhere to invite us for a drink at the famous Carlton Terrace. It was 5 p.m., the time when celebrities have their cup of tea, pralines and cookies, and a bit of chitchat.

The Carlton Terrace is an-open air eatery. It is a pleasant place to have a nice drink. But it is actually much more than that. It's where the world's rich and famous lounge around for a sip and a view. To be viewed that is. So we did just that.

Gisele and Jean Paul were suitably impressed and kept giving me those "he's a Carlton Terrace type of guy" looks. Over the years, I've grown to like such looks coming my way. They massage my ego no end. And make me feel like someone I'm obviously not.

It was inevitable, really. The simple truth is that the Carlton isn't just a place to sleep in. It isn't just a grand "palace" hotel. It isn't just an iconic institution. It's far beyond such ordinary terms. It's a place where the world wants to meet and be seen. It's the place where you want to book a suite if you happen to own, say, a company like the Fiat, or Ford, or Mitsubishi, or IBM, or a chain of five thousand department stores worldwide, or some oil wells in some shimmering desert. It's the place to make friends with movie stars and, of course, there's no better occasion than the Cannes Film Festival for that.

Just before leaving their hotels to see the films, the privileged guests milled about in the lobby. The action started right here, and the atmosphere was electric when I happened to drop in. At the Carlton, this is almost a subculture. It's a scene straight from the classics. Between the lobby's four white pillars, the stars gather around, air-kissing everyone, exchanging news and views and indulging in a bit of gossip. There were actors, actresses, directors, producers and just plain, ordinary billionaires. The gentlemen looked from "super to semi-dapper" in dark suits and tuxedos, as is the custom to dress for the Cannes Film Festival. However, it is the ladies I need to mention. But what can I say? To say that they were dressed up is an absurd understatement. The fact was their attire ranged from ordinarily brilliant to extraordinarily dazzling to downright outrageous. Shiny dresses in bright colours, designed by crazy designers who probably didn't have a clue as to what they were creating. Whatever the merits of the dresses, two facts stood out. The ladies looked dazzling and radiant. And I didn't know a single one.

Everyone wants to be photographed with everyone, so whoever had a camera got busy. The gentlemen took photos. The ladies took photos. Their friends took photos and even the staff joined in to lend a helping hand. There I was, standing alone in a corner of the lobby, and so they took my photo, alone, and with assorted groups. I must admit to feeling rather smug about this. And when two gorgeous ladies in outrageous gowns asked if I would share their photo frame, my smugness turned to unbridled joy. I'd crossed the threshold of isolation. I belonged. And I didn't care if it was I or my turban that they cared for more.

I must admit I had become a part of the show. All primed up and ready. Well, almost ready. You see, there was this business of my tuxedo. Or rather of my tuxedo which wasn't there. The fact was, I didn't have one with me and Narjiss, sweetheart that she is, arranged one for me with the concierge. The lady behind the desk handed it to me as if it was a poisonous black snake. That was fine. What wasn't fine was that I couldn't get the damn bow on when I went to the rest room by the side of the lobby to wear the dress. "It's a defective piece," I told myself. "That's why the concierge handled it like it was the last deadly serpent on earth." I wrestled with the silly little wisps of cloth with the two ridiculous knots. I couldn't manage it. The hooks just wouldn't fit. People were watching me. Finally, I sought the help of the two lady attendants stationed just outside the rest rooms. With a straight face, they did the job, and I did the rest. Went through the evening with flawless ease!

Meanwhile the stars chatted, kissed and smiled, and chatted some more before making a dramatic exit through the famous door and piling into waiting, swanky limousines that included the latest luxury series of the world's top automotive companies.

If you're a car buff, just stay put here for an hour or so. You'll get to see the Mercedes 5 series, the BMW 6 series, the Audi 7 series and the Ferrari 8 series – well, you *know* what I mean. All right, I may have got some of the series mixed up, but then I never said I was a car fiend. And you know what I'm trying to get at, anyway.

I strode out of the hotel like a conquering hero and got my first glimpse of the crowds. Dusk had started to settle and given Cannes's main boulevard, La Croisette, a golden hue. The boulevard was packed to the brim with hordes of people stationed at vantage points, eager to see the stars and their lovers and companions, even their sidekicks. Anyone would do, so long as he had the Hollywood swagger. Let's be honest. If you emerge from the Carlton during the film-festival, it means you're somebody. And if you happen to be wearing a red turban, well, it adds up.

The crowds are mostly tourists, but some locals join in too. They're eager and enthusiastic, almost always well-behaved. And then there are the photographers, the worst part of the deal, and they're anything but well-behaved. Quite the opposite, in fact! Aggressive, obtrusive, almost threatening, they swoop down on anyone who looks like a prominent movie star, not-so-prominent movie star, even an unknown movie star; producer, assistant producer, director, assistant director; oil tycoon; steel tycoon; any tycoon'; royalty; aristocracy; whatever, and snap you till you're ready to drop.

They literally manhandle their subjects to get them to strike the right pose and just when you're about ready to throttle them, they give you something like a jaded smile and thrust their business cards into your hand. They can't be avoided for the simple reason that they block your way. You can't ignore them because they keep talking to you without let-up and reach out for your hands, shoulder, or any part of your anatomy that's handy in terms of getting your attention. One followed me for a hundred camera-clicking-metres before he felt he'd done his job.

Under normal circumstances, the walk from the Carlton to the Palais Des Festivals could take anything from seven to twelve minutes, depending on how much interest you take in the surroundings. My walk took some twenty minutes, not because I took any great interest in the settings that evening. I'd seen them several times before. It was just that I walked at the same pace as the other guests from the Carlton, and from other hotels too, I guess. They tend to walk at a certain pace that denotes two things – that they are someone of substance, and that they have done this before. I hadn't done this before. But then there's always a first time and besides, I'm a quick learner. I guess it's fair to say I'm quick when it comes to slowing down.

Reaching the outer periphery of the Palais Des Festivals, the stars stop for a few seconds and say something to their companions. Assuming it was the done thing here, I paused too and gave the building a good look-over. The security was airtight and we were checked four times before we reached the fabled Red Carpet.

I'd waited a long time for this little piece of snooty adventure to become a part of my life. I did everything perfectly. Walked at the right pace, took two imaginary calls on my cell phone, pretended to read an urgent message, smiled at the right times, looked back as though waiting for someone to catch up with me and paused at the right spots. I don't really know what I was expecting, but the fact is that there was no thunder and lightning, no bells chimed and much to my dismay and annoyance, no one seemed to really notice me.

It hurt. The fact was that I was just one of some twelve hundred celebrities there that evening. Me, just one of twelve hundred? It was about as sobering a thought as I'd ever had in a very long time.

A minute later I was seated at the balcony of the auditorium, watching the giant screen that showed the entire proceedings going on, focusing on the other guests arriving and doing their sauntering, strutting bit on the well-trodden path, exactly as I'd done a few minutes earlier.

A little commotion interrupted my thoughts. We all strained our necks to see who or what had happened. I suppose you can call it one of the side highlights or the high sidelights, or whatever you want. The film director Michael Hanneke staged a slow, dramatic entrance to a smattering of applause. With him were half a dozen kids featured in the movie, who moved even slower than him. They grouped and posed for the cameramen, dispersed, regrouped, dispersed again, regrouped again, and then made their way into the auditorium, to be eventually seated with some fanfare.

Then they screened the movie – *The White Ribbon* – and it was suitably long, loud (as in acoustics) and grim. It was a serious movie with a serious theme. It was in black-and-white, seemed to go on-and-on, and had copious amounts of drama, little doses of romance and plenty to depress you at least for a while. The scary thing is that I actually enjoyed it.

As things turned out, the film's drama faded in comparison to what awaited me.

Now, let me be straight with you. I'm used to being singled out for attention now and then, here and there. But it *has* happened, you know. It's happened almost everywhere around the world, in cold climes and hot. And I've got sort of used to it, and frankly, maybe enjoy it. But nothing had prepared me for what followed in the next ten minutes.

Exiting the auditorium, I found myself walking behind a group of three couples who were approached, or more accurately, accosted by the prowling photographers. They were hanging about like a pack of wolves, strategically positioned to ensure no one escaped their dragnet. They blocked the path of the three couples, took their photos, handed them their business cards and then lost interest in them.

I walked right into, and then through them and, just when I thought I'd avoided their clutches and made it to safety, one of them ran towards me, frantically waving his arm. Seeing this, two more ran up along with him, also waving and shouting something. Within a couple of seconds, they were joined by two more.

My emerging from the auditorium meant I must be somebody. And I think, the fact that I was literally the first to leave and was alone, sort of added to my mystique. Since this business of being alone has almost become the story of my life, I know what I'm talking about.

Two of them, deciding I needed close attention, blocked my path and began to "click me in". This triggered off a chain reaction whereby all the other photographers in the immediate vicinity swooped in to be in on the action, as if by remote-control. By some strange twist of fate, the word spread that I was a film director – a new wave, shadowy, maverick, anti-establishment, and very avant-garde film director. I doubt if there are too many such turbaned, maverick film directors around and so there I was. The man himself! The *director!*

"Here we go again. It's my engaging personality," I told myself, trying to dodge past the first lot. "True class shows, I suppose."

All hell broke loose. I was literally besieged. In a matter of seconds, all the immediate focus had shifted to me. They virtually ignored all other worthies – who were genuine celebrities – and surrounded me, with a level of eagerness I didn't know existed in grown men. They literally hemmed me in, their cameras clicking, heads nodding, eyes pleading, tongues wagging, their enthusiasm strong and unbridled. The wolf pack had moved in for the kill and I was in the middle of it all, at the centre of things. The flashing cameras resembled the scenes you see pertaining to world luminaries. I literally had to shield my eyes from the incessant flashing.

Now there were two human layers around me. In the inner circle were the photographers and in the outer one were the other guests at the festival, the genuine celebrities, who'd stopped to see what exactly was going on and to find out who exactly I was supposed to be. There was frenzied excitement. I was literally blockaded. Now I knew the circumstances under which Milton had devised the word "pandemonium".

I don't know exactly how long this lasted. I think it was about three minutes. Finally, they let off. After all, there were other famous folk around and they had a job to do.

My walk back to the Carlton was a dream. I seemed to be walking on air. La Croisette is always a treat and has always charmed me. Tonight, it was a peach. In my hand, there were some two dozen business cards the photographers had literally thrust upon me. I later found a few in my coat pocket too. I reached the Carlton and stood for a moment to admire its famous façade from my vantage point on the famous promenade. Entering the hotel, I paused, or should I say posed in the lobby, expecting, I don't quite know what. To be honest, I'd got a bit used to being noticed and harried and gently jostled around. Being completely ignored was new to me. I felt strange walking in all by myself, to my room.

The next morning Narjiss asked me how it had gone. "Oh, it was fabulous. Thank you so much. The movie was nice, the whole occasion pleasant and I was mobbed by the cameramen." I paused to let all this sink in. "They must have mistaken me for someone else," I added modestly.

Narjiss gave me one of her famous, devastating smiles. "Who would they mistake *you* for Inder? They just liked you."

Shortly after that, I narrated my story to my dear friends Gisele and Jean Paul, who'd driven down to see me. "I'm not surprised," Gisele said to me with a deadpan expression on her face. "Look at it this way. These photographers are used to seeing super celebrities during the Cannes Film Festival. But they've probably never encountered one with a turban." But I was not a film director or any other kind of celebrity either, I said.

"Yes of course, you aren't. We know that, everyone else who knows you, knows that. But they don't. Besides, you do have this certain, if I may say so, enigmatic look about you that makes you look mysterious and important. Let them fantasize about you if it makes them happy. Why worry about it?

Why, indeed?

3

Malaysia, Truly Nostalgia

Every time I've visited Malaysia, I've secretly hoped to bump into Michelle Yeo. Yes, *the* Michelle Yeo, that gorgeous woman who's charmed millions of men in her movies and who used say in the tourism advertisement about Malaysia being her home. With three visits to the country completed and no chance meeting with Michelle, or anyone else as glamorous as her, you'd have thought I'd be a bit disgruntled about this particular aspect about her home. But the fact is that I'm not. On the contrary, I've developed a soft corner for this Asian cultural melting-pot. Melting-pot it certainly is, thanks to its mix of population that comprises Malays, Chinese and Indians.

Thanks to a little gentle persuasion from Chandra Sehagran of Tourism Malaysia, I found myself in the delightful environs of Malaysia's East Coast, where the wind blows strong and the waters of the South China Sea lap the shores with varying degrees of force. This region is still relatively fresh in the sense that mass tourism hasn't overcome it as yet. Which makes it more attractive, alluring and quite worth the effort of visiting.

We'd driven out of Kuala Lumpur in the morning, eased into the countryside, traversed varied landscapes, and arrived at the East Coast area, not quite knowing what to expect. Which, in my book, is the way travel really should be.

Our first stop was the Club Med Cherating Beach, and this being my first Club Med experience, as they call it, I was somewhat unprepared for the quantity, diversity and intensity of leisure action they unleash on guests. They grab hold of you, come at you thick and fast, and ensure things happen at frenzied pace and keep happening till you're ready to say "pina colada ooh la dada". The fact that *I* didn't say "pina colada ooh la dada" simply means that no amount of action is enough for me, but that's another story.

I found myself blending in rather well in rather a short period of time. The place is dreamy enough. They obviously chose the site with care. Straddling a magnificent golden beach, sprawled across a vast stretch, the resort is a splayed-out affair, with all the structures made of wood. In fact they boast they have the longest wood structure and corridor in the world. With its bungalows perched on stilts nestling among luxurious vegetation, the 197-acre resort is full of the sounds of macaws, gibbons, giant lizards, rare species of birds and multicoloured butterflies. Not to mention the guests who can be seen in various hues and have a rhythm of their own. Like most leisure guests in most resorts around the world, they seemed to be swarming all over the place, all the time. There's something going on round-the-clock. Sitting by the swimming pools, you can see the world go by – at least in leisure terms. The guests come from different continents and are of different ages.

Two restaurants– one an open buffet and the other a fine-dining outlet, cater to all manner of culinary needs. The buffets are elaborate affairs comprising assorted cuisine that includes everything from Malaysian to Chinese and Indian. The idea behind the culinary plan is to ensure that every guest finds something to his liking on the table. Beer, beverages and soft drinks are on tap. For those seeking a little privacy, there's a spacious lounge that offers a quiet environment not found elsewhere in the resort. And then there's their watering hole – the main bar that's large enough to entertain a hundred thirsty patrons. Not surprisingly, this place has a high amount of activity for most of the day and late into the night, as I found out.

If overtaken by guilt, thanks to minor bouts of overeating, hit the gym and kid yourself into believing you've shed more calories than you've imbibed. There's nothing illegal or immoral about such fantasizing. Most gyms worldwide survive and thrive on such silly, fanciful theories. They've got everything in terms of gadgetry to put you back in shape. This done, shed some more guilt by stopping by at the sports centre located out in the open and haul away at tennis or whatever.

Over the years, I've developed a tendency to try to notice as much as possible, wherever and whenever possible and file it all away in my mind. As a travel journalist, this has been a huge asset to my writing. Here, things were about ideal as they could be. I really had nothing to do apart from just taking it easy and observing everything I could around me.

More than the guests, it was the staff that I tended to observe. Hailing from fourteen countries, they were a truly motley lot. According to Club Med work tradition, the staff also takes care of the numerous activities that range from singing, joining you at your table for a meal, edging up to you at the bar for some friendly chit chat and performing on stage. In fact, their stage performance smacked of a degree of professionalism that would do credit to the famed floor shows of Paris. The show I saw certainly didn't lack anything in terms of pure zest and enthusiasm.

A young boy and girl from the staff accosted me after lunch and asked if they could take up a little of my time. The boy was from the Philippines and the girl from Japan. Both happened to be doing a sort of thesis on world civilizations and wanted to know something about the history of Sikhism. They just about knew that there was a religion called Sikhism and that was it, they admitted sheepishly. Would I care to enlighten them?

I readily agreed to their request and we found a quiet corner on the beach and sat ourselves down. Within a minute, as if by magic, we were joined by two other girls who asked if they could listen in. A few minutes later, another girl appeared out of nowhere. And so my audience swelled. As we talked, I could see all of them getting more interested in the proceedings. I gave them all the information and facts I could remember about the Sikh religion, from its origin and history to its salient features. For good measure, I mentioned my own personal sense of pride and delight at being a Sikh.

One thing was for sure. I'd got their undivided attention. The Japanese girl's face was glowing and I could see that she was literally bursting with curiosity, but holding back because of politeness. On my telling her she could go right ahead and ask me whatever she wanted, the floodgates opened and she posed question after question. Taking their cue from that, the others joined in, and there was a flurry of questions. It was almost like an interview, mildly exhausting but highly pleasant. When the hour-long session came to an end, they thanked me profusely and we went our separate ways.

I was later told by Chandra that my little study group had attracted considerable attention and interest among the resort's guests. Chandra has a sense of humour and a witty side to him and this manifests rather starkly during our travels. "You were quite a rage out there, man," he said with a grin. I won't deny feeling a bit smug at all this, but the fact is that I *was* quite a rage, as Chandra had put it and with good reason. After all, it wasn't every day that a Club Med resort saw a turbaned man addressing a bevy of pretty young girls on a pristine stretch of beach. When I told him that I was merely telling the girls a bit about my religion, he gave me one of those "oh yeah, of course" type of looks. He then grinned again and shook his head as if he'd given up on me. Which of course, made me think of all the people around the world who have, sort of "given up" on me!

The next afternoon was without incident. Twenty-four hours had flown by and it was time to say farewell to this lively place and its energetic, friendly staff. As it often happens to me, I was sad to leave.

A ceremonial send-off and we hit the road, bound for Kuala Trengganu, our jump-off point for Redang Island. Our quick lunch at a traditional café was a real treat because it served as many as three of my rather long list of favourite dishes – mildly spiced thin chicken curry, deep fried fish, and spicy salad. It was a real treat.

An hour's ferry ride and we reached Redang Island and alighted at Sari Pacifica Resort. The sun was shining, the waves lapped the golden beach gently and the seabed glistened. All the trappings of paradise were at hand and as always, I was ready.

Arriving almost at the same time as us was a boatload of other guests that included a group of three young women. They seemed friendly and we waved at one another the way silly tourists do at exotic places around the world. I learnt later that one of them was Malaysian and the other two lived in Hong Kong. For want of anything more appropriate at the time, I dubbed them the "group of three".

The resort was everything it's said to be. What's on offer is high quality stuff. The resort sprawls across one of the world's finest sea-face areas, providing views worth a hundred glances. Three islands stand as sentinels against the blue expanse of the sky and sea. Green, blue and turquoise – the water seemed as still as a millpond, touching the golden sand on the beach almost delicately. Somehow, that stuck in my mind – the fact that the water was so gentle. No waves, no seagulls, no sound. Just a pretty stillness.

The long, golden stretch of beach is common property and shared with other resorts. And the structure itself is of imposing proportions, with an impressive façade and seems to have been conceived with dreamy holidays in mind.

In a way, I'd been forewarned about the seduction by none other than Tan Sri Datuk Seri Panglima Abdul Kadir bin Haji Sheikh Fadzir, former Malaysian Tourism Minister and currently Executive Chairman, Sazean Group, which operates quality resorts in Malaysia. So I was expecting something special. In his inimitable, charming manner, Tan Sri Fadzir had revealed the true strength of the Sari Pacifica brand. "It presents an authentic Malaysian experience. I think you're going to like the place and the experience," he'd said to me with a smile.

I mentioned this to Chandra and we both agreed that the praise lavished on the place was totally justified. When Chandra told me that we were all expected to maintain a certain sense of decorum here, I honestly didn't know exactly how seriously to take him and wondered what this little island possessed that would test our respectability in the first place. The place was quiet enough to put one to sleep. Still, one can always hope, I suppose. By the way, talking of sleep, I did sleep more soundly here than I've done in many places around the world. Sleep doesn't come easily to me, you see, so it's always an issue in my life.

I went exploring the place. The spa sported a tranquil atmosphere. The conference room looked like a nice place in which to conduct a meeting. The guest rooms are split into two lots – on the beachfront and clustered around a lily pond. Pathways hive off in all directions. The afternoon went by quickly, as often happens in exotic places.

Sunset brought with it a beautiful package of its own. Sunsets always breed nostalgia in me and make me a bit sad. Sunsets in paradise are heady stuff and I guess I haven't quite managed to cope with them.

"Yes, life is complex, and so are emotions. And things can get lonely if you're alone in exotic locales like this one," Chandra said to me in a matter-of-fact tone that suggested a bit of experience of life. "But that's the way things are." "Yes, that's the way things tend to be," I replied, trying to inject some personal experience of my own into my tone. We both lapsed into silence for a while, digesting this vital statement's portents.

"Oh, by the way, did I ever tell you that fishing is my passion?" Chandra was looking more excited than I'd ever known him to be. "No, you didn't. What with one thing or another, it must have slipped your mind." "I try to take in some fishing wherever the opportunity presents itself and there's excellent fishing here. I'm contemplating going out to the sea for some deep-sea fishing tonight. You're welcome to join me if you like."

He explained his great interest in the sport, and how he wanted to try his luck here. Who knows, he might land a big catch. He was hiring a boat to take him out to sea. "How big a boat?" I asked, trying to sound and look casual. I couldn't help remembering the film *Jaws* and Richard Dreyfuss saying, "You're going to need a bigger boat," when he caught his first glimpse of the infamous Great White Shark that made the film a classic and started a universal phobia about sharks. But Chandra was quite unfazed. "Oh, big enough," he said with a grin. You can't pull one over Chandra that easily. "A boat is a boat," he added with an impish grin.

As things transpired, eventually he went on his own in his "big enough" boat and as he told me later, had quite an outing though he didn't manage to land a big fish. I think it was something to do with the sea being too choppy or something like that. But he did manage to indulge in his passion and that's what I believe life should be all about.

Sari Pacifica Resort is idyllic in more ways than one. It's a place for those who are smart enough not to waste time in their rooms. You can do so much – snorkel, scuba dive, deep-sea dive, fish, swim, island-hop, watch turtles, laze around, eat and drink. It's a lot of tough choices, if you ask me. So you can be smart and do what I did. Laze around, eat and drink.

Justice done to this wonderful resort, it was time to sail out to discover the other gems of the island. And they don't come any prettier than Sari Pacifica Resort & Spa, Lang Tengah Island, a resort that seems tailor-made for diehard escapists, honeymooners and all those not sure of what they want from a holiday.

Here it was scuba-diving time. Everyone took the plunge except me, but then, as I was at pains to explain to anyone willing to listen, someone has to stay back and look after things while the boys and girls go out and frolic. Besides, there was also this little business of the beer to be guarded. Never let it be said that I shirked my duty.

The girls, or should I say, the "group of three" had enjoyed diving and frolicking around in the water and had returned to the boat – with a helping hand from the dutiful guard. They seemed to be in a particularly good mood and chatted alternately among themselves and with me. They asked if I'd mind being photographed with them and I agreed, with the speed and grace I've perfected when asked such things by pretty women and we duly asked Chandra if he'd be kind enough to be the photographer. To his credit, let it be said that he did a wonderful job, though at one point he did call me a "clever, scheming devil".

"Look here, what's going on here?" he asked me with a half-smile just before we were leaving the island. "For the past three days you've been a hit with the women. If your 'study class' with the Club Med girls wasn't enough, now this lot here is taking undue interest in you. I hope you won't get carried away and forget why we came here in the first place. It's plain for the world to see that all these women seem unduly attracted by your turban. And you seem to be rather pleased with all this."

"Of course I'm pleased," I told him grandly. "Wouldn't you be, in my place? But don't worry. I have a job to do and will do it sincerely, steadfastly and dutifully. My writings on Malaysia will flow smoothly. I won't let the 'turban factor' affect my concentration."

I didn't. But it did affect several young women's concentration, and that certainly did affect mine too.

4

Auckland, Actually

"It's a big city, but then there are other big cities around the world," Sharon had told me with a firm look in her eyes.

But Sharon lives in Wellington and folks down there don't really like Auckland. "We have this sort of rivalry you see," she added softly. "The fact is that I'm feeling a little possessive about you and don't want you getting too fond of Auckland."

Well, fine, I told myself. As the good woman had admitted to feeling a little possessive towards me just hours after we'd met up, I felt she deserved my attention. My fond attention. The fact that she was pretty and friendly made my fond resolve that much stronger.

What can you say about a city that's got a fourth of the entire country's population, except that it is big, bustling and booming? Home to over a million people, Auckland is New Zealand's largest city and commercial hub, with the world's largest concentration of Polynesian people.

There's an interesting background to the region. In the Maori language, Auckland is known as Tamaki Makau Rau, the maiden with a hundred lovers, a name earned because it was a place desired by all and conquered by many. A brief visit was enough to told me why.

Legend has it that the city's first inhabitants were the magical, fair-skinned Turehu people who cultivated its rich soil. While all Maori iwi (tribes) of the region claim to have descended from the Turehu, their tribal identities are generally linked to the ancestral waka that sailed to New Zealand from Hawaiiki – the legendary homeland of the Maori on the Pacific island.

In the mid-18th century, invaders from the Ngati Whatua iwi conquered Auckland. Captain James Cook's chartering of New Zealand's coastline in 1769 missed Waitemata Harbour but he left behind several names for places, such as Great Barrier and Little Barrier Islands. In 1820, Samuel Marsden became the first known European to explore the Hauraki Gulf.

Straddling an eleven-kilometre wide volcanic isthmus peppered by forty-eight dormant volcanoes and surrounded by three harbours – the Waitemata, the Manakua and the Kaipara – New Zealand's largest, modern-day Auckland stretches from the town of Wellsford in the north to the rolling Bombay Hills in the south. Administratively, it is divided into four cities – Auckland, Manukau, North Shore and Waitakere, and three districts – Franklin, Rodney and Papakura.

Today, Auckland is a city on the move, possessing just about everything a big city needs to become known. For good measure, its fertile valleys and islands produce award-winning wines.

Thirty minutes after arriving, I found myself in the delightful confines of Mollies – a story in itself. The love-child of talented the couple, Frances Wilson and Stephen Fitzgerald, Mollies is a rare treat. Frances and Stephen's passion for opera, design and fine antiques is visible in every room and with centuries-old antiques and sleek modern furniture companionably sitting side by side, their unwavering eye for beauty has resulted in a wonderfully eclectic yet soothing environment. It's a treat for the senses.

Frances took me on a guided tour of the premises, allowing me to poke my head into all of the ten odd suites, each a statement of style, each welcoming in their own way. Later, in the lounge, they played the piano just for me. Quite fittingly, I thought. The fire crackled, Polly the cat sulked, and it was all just fine, just right. Ten short steps took me to the bar with its refined elegance and breathtaking view of Auckland Bridge.

The walls are off-white with uneven grey patches, embellished by classical paintings. The upholstery is studiously plain, the curtains are classical in appearance, the tables though contrast sharply as they are green glass, modern-looking affairs. Mollies is grace and elegance personified. I couldn't have asked for a better place to stay.

The City of Sails beckoned. And the best way to appreciate it is from on the water, a local must-do. With the isthmus separating two harbours – the Waitemata and Manukau – this is a water-lover's paradise with the world's largest boat ownership per capita. That is why it is known as the City of Sails. Your on-the-water experience could be as thrilling as a white-knuckle race on board a Grand Prix racing yacht, or as laid-back as a ferry cruise to a seaside suburb or idyllic islands. There are safe swimming beaches, sheltered bays and wild surf breaks. Yes sir, this is a sea-lover's paradise.

Regular ferries service the islands of the Huaraki Gulf, which offers spectacular cruising options and is an unspoilt eco-tourism haven. It is also home to pods of dolphins and whales, best viewed on board the Dolphin Explorer. Charter boats are available in every incarnation, from classic yachts to speed launches. Take a cruise around the spectacular Waitemata Harbour, skirt the Harbour Bridge, then explore the charming and historic seaside suburb of Devonport, replete with cafes, art galleries, parks and beaches. And try not to hurry.

You can windsurf and kayak in the bays around the harbour. A thirty-minute ferry ride from downtown Auckland will land you on Rangitoto, Motutapu, Waiheke or Mothuihe. Journey a little longer and you step onto Kawau or Tiritiri, while a thirty-minute flight will get you to Great Barrier Island.

Hit the beach! This is New Zealand's most magnificent coastline. Just ten minutes from downtown, you can relax on golden sand as the protected waters of the Hauraki gulf lap gently at the shore. Then thirty minutes later, settle down on a rugged, sweeping beach on the west coast, its volcanic black sand pounded by the surf of the Tasman Sea. A can of beer would do no harm to your beach experience.

Fittingly, my first foray was out at sea, courtesy the unique SailNZ experience of sailing an America's Cup Yacht around Auckland Harbour. Having raced in the America's Cup, NZL 41 is a famous yacht that can take up to thirty passengers. Of course, you've got to pay for the ride, but believe me, it's worth every cent. You can just pay and hop aboard for a two-hour ride, become part of the crew and are encouraged to participate in steering and navigating the famous boat.

We sailed out of Viaduct Harbour – the famous venue for the America's Cup – animating with bars, bistros and restaurants. There were four handles and we handled them. That's how the sails went up. Out at sea, I remember thinking what a pity it was that so many building cranes all over the place spoilt the Auckland skyline view. But that apart, it was *some* view.

By the time the second sail came up we were doing a fair clip of ten knots. The wind was 11-11.5. I took the steering wheel for a bit and immediately felt it to be better than driving my car along Delhi's crowded roads. We didn't encounter too many boats in the harbour area, but did see a rather squat looking, ugly boat that was used for tackling killer whales.

It was an outing to cherish, and the ride was everything it is made out to be.

From dramatic lava landscapes to sunlit olive groves, uninhabited white sandy beaches to wildlife sanctuaries and marine reserves, each island in the region has a different character. The waters that separate the islands are home to pods of dolphins, families of blue penguins and the occasional pod of Orca, as the killer whales are known.

Come evening, and Tessa Lawrence of Tourism New Zealand decided I needed to do the conventional city drive-about. Taking the "scenic route", we passed Queen Street, the main shopping area, and were briefly dwarfed by the imposing girth of Skycity as we did the Central Business District.

The city is home to the Sky Tower, the tallest building in the southern hemisphere. In 1998, the world's highest bungie jump was made from the tower, and now paying thrill-seekers can jump off the tower for a unique experience. One can also climb over and under and jump from the spectacular Harbour Bridge. As it happens, this is the only harbour bridge jump in the world.

Ten minutes later, we stood at the Auckland Museum, an impressive sandstone coloured granite building squatting on a low hill, featuring an excellent frontage and wonderful views. Then we wound our way to Mount Eden near the central city for even better, 360-degree views across both the Pacific and Tasman coasts. All of Auckland lay sprawled below us as we stood at the summit and braved the wind.

Often voted one of the world's best lifestyle cities, Auckland adopts outdoors buffs with a 37,000 hectares network of regional parks, farm parks, parks with archaeological sites, historic homesteads, marine reserves and botanic gardens. There are hiking trails in the Waitakere and Hunua Ranges that take you into cool, peaceful rainforests. The Woodhill and Riverhead plantation forests attract mountain bikers and motorcross riders. And there are over thirty golf courses, including famous ones like those at Gulf Harbour and Formosa.

I realized that feeling hungry in the city is a matter of good luck. There's simply so much to taste and relish here that trying out the local cuisine is another must-do.

Auckland has perfected the cuisine style called "Pacific Rim", that blends Asian and Pacific flavours. Seafood features prominently on menus. Try New Zealand green lipped mussels, succulent Clevedon Coast oysters, or the local lamb or venison. Exciting dining options ranging from international cuisine to takeaway gourmet burgers exist at the historic inner-city suburbs of Ponsonby, Herne Bay and Parnell. Parnell is a dining institution with perennial favourites like Iguacu, Metropole and Parnell Institution Cibo. Go to a waterfront restaurant in the Viaduct Harbour or Mission Bay. Or go picnicking with a steaming parcel of fish-and-chips at a peaceful beach or bay, or try some fresh bread-and-cheese selection from the Puhoi Valley.

Complimenting the food are several award-winning wines from some eighty local wineries. Waiheke Island's Stonyridge is famous for its reds and produces Larose, one of the world's top twenty Cabernet blends. The west and north-west areas boast old wineries and Clevedon and Matakana are also noteworthy wine areas. Look for admired labels such as Kumeu River, Stonyridge and Matua Valley. Several vineyards have good in-house restaurants that offer "fine dining among the grapes".

After dinner, take a look at the local nightlife. Lively bars and pubs proliferate the central city, with the big dance clubs centred on Karangahape Road, known locally as K Road. The local casino, bars, restaurants, and a hotel make up the Skycity Auckland complex, a lively one-stop leisure venue. Live music and theatre are featured in large venues such as the Aotea Centre, the Bruce Mason Theatre and Skycity Theatre, while the Civic Theatre on Queen Street has been restored to its art deco glory.

Two days had rushed by in a blur. I dare say I hadn't wasted a minute while in the city. I saw and did a lot. But I did come away with the feeling that there was still a lot to see and do in this charming city by the sea.

5

An Omani Interlude

The very term "Arabia" has always struck a chord in my memory. Floating into my mind has been an amalgam of thoughts which have included everything from magic carpets to desert sunsets, camel safaris, and hardy tribesmen.

All right, diehard romantic that I am, I could be accused of adding just that little bit of hype to things, but the fact is that Arabia is a special sort of a place, and the Arab world does have its own rhythm and beat.

By and large, the Arabs are proud, traditional, deeply religious people. Many facets of life in the Arab world are different from those prevalent in other parts of the world. This stems largely from local, regional, religious, cultural and social norms. Accepting and respecting these norms is not only considered to be in good taste, but also something expected from foreign guests.

The first of my various trips to Oman came courtesy of the Oman Embassy in New Delhi. I had befriended a gentleman named Hasan who was attached to the Embassy as a diplomat and he arranged my visit to his country in my capacity of a travel journalist. A fine gentleman, Hasan was justifiably proud of his country. "You'll like Oman," he'd said simply, but with a tone full of enthusiasm.

As it turned out, Hasan was right. I did like Oman. My trip and stay in the country provided me with a glimpse of Arab lifestyle and enlightened me about the fact that the Omanese, while as religious and traditional as the rest of the Arab world, are basically easy-going, good-hearted people with a progressive bent of mind and want to move ahead along with the rest of the world. They also have a great sense of humour. And once you earn their respect, they're willing to go the extra mile for you.

As a guest of the Oman Government, I'd been received and welcomed by a gentleman named Darwish who worked for the Oman Information Ministry. Taking care of visiting journalists was one of his responsibilities and he did a good job of it. He turned out to be a fine gentleman with a subtle sense of humour. In fact, you will encounter many fine gentlemen in Oman.

A part of my itinerary included courtesy calls and meetings with very senior government executives in Muscat. Three prominent executives who I remember well were Engr. Abdullah bin Abbas bin Ahmed, Head of Muscat Municipality and President – Municipal Council; Ali Mohamed Za'abnoot, Director General of Information; and Salim bin Adey Al-Mamari, Oman's Director General of Tourism Promotion. All three came across as very knowledgeable, dignified and courteous and all of them were striving and working for a progressive future for their country. They were very clear in their thinking and quickly translated their thoughts into action. I learnt a little about their country's culture from my visits to their offices.

Engr. Abdullah told me that they wanted to open up the country to visitors, further develop their infrastructure, and improve the overall quality of their products. He gave me some information about the Muscat Festival, which was launched in 1998, in conjunction with the Ministry of Tourism with the objective of encouraging tourists to visit Oman. The purpose was to showcase Oman's culture and heritage and create a momentum for the future. As I found, the festival had done just that, and also provided a platform for locals to intermingle and enjoy some family fun.

Za'abnoot mentioned that Oman was moving ahead on a dual mission that includes combining heritage and culture, while simultaneously progressing and transforming. The idea was to maintain their traditions and culture, while going for more education, technology and human resource development. It was a fine balance, that was benefiting the country and its citizens.

Al-Mamari felt Oman had several unique selling points, such as safety, cleanliness, a quiet environment, ability to offer a unique historical and cultural experience; scenery, and the bounties of nature. With all this backed up by a good infrastructure, the country's tourism potential was enormous and they were keen to promote it for ecology, adventure and health tourism, to mention a few key areas.

As per the local hospitality custom, I was offered coffee in the three offices. Once you finish your coffee, an attendant will replenish your glass and if you're done, you're supposed to shake the empty glass a couple of times, upon which he'll take it away. Not knowing this, I hanged on to my glass the way a relay sprinter does to a baton and saw it duly refilled thrice, before finally giving it up. No one said anything, of course, but I later learnt that it's considered polite to have one, or maximum two helpings. A bit embarrassed, I filed this helpful tip away in the corner of my mind, for the future. That's the whole charm of travelling. You learn a lot that you'd never learn sitting at home.

While the coffee is standard, sometimes you're also offered *halwa* – a kind of thick pudding that always tastes good. With halwa being a household item in India, and taking pride of place among my rather long list of personal favourites, I knew my way around in this particular field. I dare say, I followed proper etiquette and did fair justice to wherever was offered to me. The fact is that I found it to be utterly delicious – in fact among the best I'd ever tasted – but mindful of my coffee episode, I was highly circumspect and daintily took just one spoonful.

With a deadpan expression on his face, Darwish told me that halwa is considered good for men. "It's good for, well, you know what? You should take some more." He was grinning from ear-to-ear and seemed hugely pleased with himself. Partly to humour him and, to be honest, partly because of what he'd said, I promptly took some more. "Oh, now you've taken too much." His grin had grown bigger and from the corner of my eye I noticed a couple of other people in the room had also overheard and seemed quite amused at what was going on. I don't know what made me say it, but say it I did and with my chest puffed out, at that. "Oh, in my community there's no such thing as too much." I now tried my version of an ear-to-ear grin.

There was complete silence for a few seconds and then everyone laughed out. By now I'd begun to feel acutely embarrassed about these events, but the deed was done, the words said and the moment gone. Anyway, it was all done in zest, and the halwa was delicious. And whether it is coffee, halwa or a bit of male chauvinism, I can never be accused of being a bad sport.

Mindful of the fact that I was visiting in my capacity as a travel journalist, I now turned my attention to the destination itself.

Ranked amongst the world's cleanest and least cluttered, Muscat is a city that you will perceive as per your personal preferences. Some may find it a bit staid, while some will definitely see and appreciate the positive attributes on offer. Having managed to do exactly that, my perception is that it is a fine city in several senses of the word.

The city is actually all about wide-open spaces, architecturally – pleasing buildings and landscaped gardens that form a neat patchwork. It offers a good quality of lifestyle to its residents. And for those who know where to find them, there are interesting old stories of former romantic times, still doing the rounds.

Once a thriving, strategically located port on the Arabian peninsula, Muscat today presents an interesting blend of the old and the new It is home to some 500,000 inhabitants and is the capital and hub of government machinery. It is also a bustling commercial centre Giving a distinct character to the city are the picturesque old buildings co-existing with modern commercial and residential quarters. The impressive cityscape of concrete and parks is dominated by pale white structures that seem to be freshly painted. The city mirrors different images ranging from contemporary to some journeying back to its founding 900 years ago. Images of old shipyards where the famous dhows were built which sailed the seas in those early days. There are many old structures like the two Portuguese forts, Jelali and Merani, that flank the rocky cove around which the city is built.

I didn't get around to hearing any old, romantic stories, but bumped into a wonderful brother-and-sister couple, who originally hailed from Lebanon. The lady's name was Lara and her brother was Abdul. And I didn't have to take even three steps from my hotel to meet them either. We just happened to meet in the lounge of the Inter-Continental where I was staying, started to chat and before you could say "misty mornings and magic carpets" we'd become friends. It's amazing how one can get friendly with some people so quickly. We strolled across to the coffee shop and made ourselves comfortable.

Describing Lara is like dabbling in poetry. She was very pretty, dignified and courteous. And she had a constant, mischievous look in her eyes. Abdul, on the other hand, had a stern disposition and I couldn't help wondering if he had ever smiled in his life.

The three of us instantly hit off and we felt totally relaxed with one another. We talked and laughed like long-lost friends. Mindful of the fact that Arabs are very conservative, I didn't know if it was proper to talk too much with Lara and so directed much of my conversation to Abdul. It was a bit funny, really! While I was ostensibly talking to both of them, I would look only at Abdul. They both noticed this, but seemed fine with it.

Initial introductions and pleasantries over, they sort of "commented" that my profession of being a travel journalist must have made my life very eventful and interesting. They both admitted that they envied me, especially as they also liked to travel and explore but didn't get too many opportunities.

Taking this as my cue, I regaled them with stories of my international travels, experiences, adventures and misadventures. The fact is that I'm very good at telling people about all the things I've done, almost all over the world. Of course, I focus on the points I *want* to focus on, and completely ignore others. But that's all right. I'm only human!

They listened intently and seemed quite taken up, but I didn't want to overdo it. Telling Lara that I could talk forever but didn't want to bore them, I asked them to take over and tell me the story of *their* lives. They looked at each other, and after a momentary hesitation, proceeded to do just that. And boy, did they talk!

Lara told me about her childhood years in Beirut and the wonderful times she had there, about her education in America and about her passion for nature. "Do you like gardening?" she asked me suddenly, and then said in a sort of resigned manner, "No, of course, you probably don't." Just as I was about to say that while I personally wasn't into gardening, I did have this liking tucked away somewhere in the back of my mind for plants and herbs and such stuff, she raised her hand. "Don't. Just don't. Don't say anything just because you feel you have to, because you *don't*. You don't have to say anything just to please me. That spoils everything. Men who do that annoy me immensely. It's really quite unnecessary. And anyway, you of all people don't have to like gardening. I shouldn't have brought it up." She took a deep breath and so did I.

Right then, at that particular moment, she looked like a little lost girl. But she instantly regained her composure and carried on. She told me about how upset her parents were that she still wasn't married and how angry they'd been when she'd turned down all the marriage proposals that had come via her family. She looked me squarely in the eyes, and in that one, fleeting moment I felt something frighteningly strong tug at my heart. I just smiled and instinctively reached out and patted her hand softly. It was a spontaneous, harmless act but one I immediately regretted. I didn't know exactly how much of a liberty I'd taken even with this small gesture, considering I was in a conservative environment and some things are just not done there. Arabs are very conservative and there are certain ground rules that apply when one meets Arab women. Afraid that I might have overstepped the limit and caused offence, I quickly withdrew my hand and apologized. I wanted to kick myself for my transgression.

There was also this gnawing thought at the back of my mind about what she'd said about I of all people not needing to like gardening. What had she meant by that? I mean, why should I of all people not have to like gardening? What was so different about me? What if I *wanted* to like gardening? Somewhere in the corner of my mind, I felt a vague discomfort at the thought, and the fact that I couldn't pinpoint the discomfort, made it worse.

Neither of them seemed to have taken offence at my little physical gesture, which was a big relief. And then the unthinkable happened. Abdul actually smiled. And started to talk! About his education to become an engineer, his passion for aeronautics and flying and his great wish to own his own aircraft one day in the not-too-distant future. This was obviously something very close to his heart because he actually smiled again.

Lara and Abdul spoke briefly with each other in Arabic and then both smiled together. I knew something was up and a conspiracy was afoot. Their broad smiles indicated it was something they thought of as being pleasant. Ceremony dictated that, as the man, Abdul take the lead. He hesitated for a few seconds, and then clearing his throat nervously, asked me if I had only one wife or more.

Priding myself with being reasonably smart and quick on the uptake, I nevertheless, was at a loss for words for a few seconds. "Oh, we didn't want to be rude," Abdul said with concern writ large on his forehead. I told him they hadn't been rude at all and it was fine. And then told them I was single.

For the first time since we'd met, Lara's expression became serious and the mischief went out of her eyes. She looked like she'd just seen a ghost. And as for Abdul, his elusive, rare smile seemed to have got locked up in a steel chest and the key thrown away.

We were one serious threesome there, locked in serious thought. Suddenly, the coffee-shop looked much bigger and considerably quieter. A few minutes later, we said goodbye to one another, parted company and went our separate ways.

By a strange coincidence I bumped into the two again at exactly the same spot some three hours later and we ended up seated together for a coffee for the second time that day.

From the moment I met them the second time, I knew there was something on their minds. It was obvious they had been discussing me. I had a feeling they wanted to talk to me about something definite While Lara was the more open of the two, being a lady it not appropriate she take the initiative in talking with a man, and so the generally quiet Abdul became their spokesperson.

"My sister and I greatly enjoyed meeting and talking to you earlier today, and we were talking about you later, after we'd parted company. We felt we could talk freely with you and if it's all right with you, would like to ask your opinion about a few things," said Abdul, a little formally. I sensed hesitancy in Abdul's voice. He glanced at Lara as if for some sort of reassurance. She nodded ever so slightly and this was his cue to continue. "We're a little intrigued by you. While you've travelled so much and seen the world as a travel journalist, and seem to know so much, you said you're single. This means you're into some deep form of spirituality, or else why would you endure a solitary existence? So we're keen to take advantage of your company and learn a few things."

Now here was a situation! Two young Arabs had mistaken me for some sort of minor spiritual guru and were soliciting my advice. Over the years, I'd had hordes of people asking me myriad questions about myself, my work, religion and existence, but I had never ever thought myself to be spiritual. Food for thought!

"Oh, I don't know if my being single makes me spiritual at all, but if there's anything on which I can enlighten you, or help out in any way, I'll be glad to." They both looked visibly relieved and unburdened themselves.

Lara spoke first and in a roundabout sort of way expressed a general sense of discontentment in life. Nothing, according to her, seemed to interest or excite her. Now it was Abdul's turn. He said that he was totally confused and didn't know what he wanted to do in life, whether to pursue his love for flying or take up some other career.

Donning a serious expression that I thought conveyed the right things – whatever they may be – I grandly told them that I could sort their dilemma quite easily. I started off by mentioning that, while they didn't know it, they both seemed to be burdened by the same problems, and so my magic formula was the same for both. Seeing that I'd got their undivided attention, I strode on.

"Let me start by mentioning that you two aren't the only individuals on this planet who appear lost and confused.

There are millions of fine people in hundreds of fine places who shared this predicament. What you're going through is what millions of men and women go through. It's a well-trodden path." I kept my tone low as befitted a spiritual person and could see that they were totally enraptured.

I carried on. "In such scenarios, sometimes the best course of action is no-action. Or taking a break, take stock and then starting all over again. Make a completely new beginning. A completely fresh start!" The truth was that I'd just said this because it was the first thing that came to my mind. But it had a dramatic effect on both of them.

They seemed lost in thought and then seemed to have come to a conclusion. "Oh, that's brilliant. Yes, that's what I should do. That's what I *will* do. Isn't it great how quickly you've found a solution to my dilemma? Honestly, this would never ever have occurred to me." Lara was smiling and seemed visibly more relaxed.

Abdul echoed her sentiments and even gave us the benefit of one of his rare smiles. I remember thinking at the time how impactful a few innocuous words could be, given the right circumstances. We chatted on for a bit and then said goodbye and I parted company with this brother-sister duo for the second time in a few hours.

The next day was taken up by my attempts at discovering some of Muscat's charms. Ever the host and guide, Darwish started off our city tour from its undisputed showpiece, the seaside palace of H.M. Sultan Qaboos bin Said. Nestled between steep rocky hills, the stately palace sports a grand building with an impressive façade and huge multi-coloured columns that feature different architectural styles and presents a spectacular sight both from the sea and land. Visitors aren't allowed in without prior permission, but I had a wonderful view of the palace and its front gardens from the gate. Every visitor to the city stops here for a photo with his companion, but there really was no one for me to be photographed with, so I skipped that part.

Also magnificent is the Al Bustan Palace Hotel, a symbol of national pride. Originally built as a guest-house for Heads of State and the Sultans of the Gulf States, the hotel offers an enticing blend of luxury hospitality and Middle-East culture in fairy-tale opulence. Set against a dramatic mountain background on 200 acres of private beach and lush green gardens, the hotel enjoys beautiful views of the Gulf of Oman. The magnificent structure spells sheer luxury through its impressive lobby, upscale dining areas and luxurious rooms. The tone is set even before one enters the spacious gardens. Perched on the roundabout at the hotel's entrance is the Sohar, the ship that sailed to China several years ago on the fabled silk route.

Designed by J&A Phillipou (Oman), the hotel's imposing Islamic lines are complemented by a luxuriously appointed Arab-style interior, designed around a central atrium with a three-tiered fountain. Your first entry into the building is an experience that stays with you. Large enough to hold a Boeing 747 standing on its nose, the atrium lobby must rank as one of, if not *the* world's most ornate and opulent. It is 33 metres high —equal in total height to the jebel that was blasted away and occupied the area of the atrium. It dwarfs you not just because of its high domed ceiling with its white, inlay rotunda, but also its overall impact. It is high luxury, plain and simple.

It was now time to see another aspect of Muscat and I got an exposure to genuine local flavour in Muttrah, a busy commercial centre renowned for its cornice; its harbour with romantic old dhows, visiting cruise ships and naval vessels; and the smells of the sea. The afternoon slipped by as we meandered through the complex maze of the market souk with its seemingly endless corridors of stalls and shops, waded through stalls of vegetables and dates and saw the day's catch on display in the busy fish souk. Munching on ripe dates and sipping mildly spiced herbal tea, I discovered why Arabian shopping can be delightful, exciting and tiring. A wealth of hand-crafted jewellery, antiques and assorted foodstuffs from the world over, besides silver coffee pots, tribal rugs, and khanjars (curved ceremonial daggers), are just some among the staggering variety of items available in the souks, which also offer a typical market-day oriented atmosphere, with noise, bargaining and plenty of head-shaking. In Souq Al Juma, popularly known as Friday Market, you can pick up new and old items from a bewildering range that includes everything from furniture to cars. In Al Qurm, elegant shopping malls beckon visitors and though the bargaining decreases, the atmosphere remains the same.

The next day Lara contacted me and asked if we could meet for a while. I instantly agreed and she was waiting dutifully for me in the hotel lobby at the appointed hour. Apparently, Abdul had gone out to meet someone. We sat ourselves down on the deckchairs on the lawns, just twenty metres from the beach. There was a gentle breeze blowing in from the sea and the tall palms splayed across the garden and lawns swayed as if in rhythm. Lara seemed excited and I had a feeling she was waiting to blurt something out.

"Can I take the liberty of asking you some personal questions?" she said to me hesitatingly. I smiled and told her she could ask whatever she wanted, in whichever way she wanted. My life was an open book.

"Actually, I want to ask three questions," she said.

"Go right ahead," I replied.

"Fine," she said softly. "Brace yourself. My questions are simple or complex, depending on how you look at them. She took a deep breath. "Here goes. Have you taken stock of your own life as you asked me to do with mine? Are you at peace with yourself and with the elements? And what do you want *most* in your life?"

There was a silence that seemed to go on and on. I wondered what to say and how to say it. I'm no stranger to awkward silences, having encountered and engendered more than a few in many different parts of the world. But somehow, this one seemed particularly unending. I may have imagined it, but I thought the wind had just got stronger and the palms swayed a lot more. I must admit I was floored by the directness and intensely personal nature of the questions. But, if I may say so, I rose to the occasion rather splendidly. Maybe the swaying palms inspired me, as I could draw a parallel between them and my wildly swaying life.

I told her that the honest truth was that I had not taken stock of my own life, at least not in a conscious or organized way. With passing years, I was beginning to think more and more about myself and my life and this included several different aspects of my existence. But I hadn't taken stock. Now that the topic had come up – and this was the first time this particular topic had come up regarding myself – the truth had dawned on me that I'd neglected this aspect completely.

Was I at peace with myself and the elements? The answer was a definite "No". The fact was that I wasn't at peace but was making a serious effort to endear myself to God. I was keen for all the blessings I could garner and was convinced that it was my only hope of survival. It wasn't just a question of salvation, but basic survival. It was my own personal, sincere quest for peace.

And what did I want most in my life? I was very clear in my own mind that while I was hungry for love, what I craved for most in my life was to be a loyalist. A total and complete loyalist to everything that mattered! My country, my family, my fraternity and most especially, my religion. What I wanted most dearly in my life was to somehow be and live life as a true Sikh, and do something constructive for Sikhism. I wanted to give something back to the religion that had given me so much.

It was only some ten seconds later that I realized the full implication of what I'd said. It also occurred to me to ask Lara why she'd asked me these questions in the first place. Something wasn't quite right. Why would a woman I just happened to meet ask me, a stranger, such direct, deeply personal questions? I accosted her with my question regarding her questions. She took a deep breath. "All right, I'll tell you. You have a right to ask this anyway. I hope you won't mind my being forthright and I hope you won't get hurt if I'm totally frank." She took another deep breath. I'd reckon it was the tenth during our conversation. "Though my brother was with me and he's very dependable and protective, when I saw you my first feeling was one of self-preservation. The first thing you reminded me of was a wolf. Don't ask me to explain it, but there's something a bit wolf-like about you. My first instinct was to protect myself from you. But your being a Sikh went hugely in your favour. My parents have had Sikh friends all through their lives and cherish their friendships and speak very highly of them. My father once told me that you could trust a Sikh to stand by you through thick-and-thin. So I told myself if you're even half the Sikh you appear be, things will be fine. To put it plainly, I trusted you. Not because of *you*, but because you're a Sikh."

She paused for a moment to see my reaction, and then continued. "There's something about you which is hard to put a finger on. While some men blow hot and cold, you seem to ebb and flow. One moment you're all there, the next moment you seem to be somewhere far, far away. And you're enigmatic. While you seem to have immense knowledge of the world in general, you seem quite naïve in many worldly matters and give the impression you're quite vulnerable. I've learnt a lot from you in our brief meetings and greatly appreciate the fact that you said what you meant. I don't doubt that for a minute. But while you were generous and selfless and gave us really good advice, I felt that the only thing you really seemed to enjoy talking about was your religion. Honestly, I got that impression. And while you come across as quite calm and composed, I feel you're plagued with all sorts of devils in your mind. You had a very good effect on both Abdul and me and helped to clear our thoughts. But I feel your own personal thoughts that pertain to yourself aren't half as clear as you'd like them to be. You look like a lost soul. A truly lost soul! About the only thing you seem to be totally comfortable with is your physical appearance – your turban and all. That's something you seem to relish. And of course, now I know why."

Once again there was a silence that seemed to go on and on. The wind was stronger than ever and the swaying palms were performing a frenzied dance. Lara and I bid our final goodbyes and once again I was alone with my thoughts. I've been in this situation at least a thousand times in my life – alone and thoughtful. There was plenty of stuff whirring about in my mind, but the thought uppermost was how Lara had read me so accurately in such a short period of time.

Right then I realized just how important my religion and physical appearance as a Sikh was to me. The feeling had always been there, but it wasn't obvious. I was happy to have it reinforced by a vivacious woman from a completely different background, with whom I'd spent just a few hours in the pristine confines of a beautiful city like Muscat.

I took it as a reminder of who I was and where I'd come from. And maybe, just maybe, where I was supposed to go.

6

Seven Days in Singapore

It was spring and my first visit to Singapore. Being a newbie in the travel writing business, I guess I tended to look at the world the way I think most young journalists do – with a sense of brashness and bravado that bordered on reckless.

I hadn't earned my stripes in the field of writing by then. Actually, I had little to show by way of professional achievement or acclaim. But this was an overseas trip – only my second overseas trip – and that made it serious business. I sensed an opportunity to achieve something through my travel writing and didn't want to miss it.

It takes just a short visit to Singapore to see that this is a place where they make things happen. Decades of systematic planning and work has ensured that local dreams become reality. What was once a fishing village is now a throbbing commercial hub, much touted as a role model of progress, development and general prosperity.

A vital junction of the Indian and Pacific Ocean and a clearing house for the region's enormous wealth, Singapore's port is among the world's busiest, with trading ships bringing all kinds of commodities from timber to coffee. Signifying industrial activity, giant oil refineries tower over the harbour. Changi International Airport has for long been ranked among the world's best. And the country ranks among the world's key financial centres.

Against this backdrop, tourism is a major industry. What they sell to tourists, and indeed what leaves a telling impression, are the experiences of incredible food, magnificent shopping and the variety of parks and leisure sites. One sees a tropical fantasy that has successfully blended stark, towering skyscrapers and quaint old Chinese shop-houses; the hubbub of commerce with the serenity of landscaped parklands; and bustling bazaars with quiet, tucked-away back-lanes. This is a near-futuristic city with the age-old abacus always at hand.

My general lack of knowledge notwithstanding, being a quick learner, I noticed several little things about Singapore. Things that later stood me in good stead during my subsequent visits and while writing on what the city was all about and what it offered to visitors. The fact is that it does offer a lot and most of it is of high standards of quality. That is one of the reasons why it has become famous throughout the world.

That everything here is spick-and-span and life disciplined, is no secret to the world. But I also noticed a sincere professional drive among the locals. When it came to business, they were as serious and committed as anyone, anywhere in the world. Their attitude blended well with the general discipline that's all-pervading here. And I feel it is this attitude that has propelled Singapore to its current heights. There is a professional efficiency in everything here.

A few years later, I ended up in Singapore again, on what turned out to be one of the most leisurely trips I've ever undertaken in my life. Frankly, it was a bit too leisurely, but then, as I've found over the years, leisure can be hard work too. Sure, I was there in my capacity as a travel journalist. But it was essentially a private visit. I was no one's guest. Which meant I had more time on my hands than I knew how to handle, which in turn, engendered a sense of loneliness in me which I also didn't know how to handle!

I dropped anchor at the Carlton Hotel on Brass Bassa Road – quite the heart of the city – and spent a week just browsing around and poking my head into various nooks and crannies, both on and off the conventional tourist map. I had the time, and certainly the inclination, and the energy levels were high.

I got into a tourist mode. Deciding to sort of hang around, I went about discovering the place at my own pace.

Within striking distance of one another is a bewildering variety of things to see and do. Take the cable car ride over the harbour to Sentosa (the name means tranquillity), with its tropical lagoon where you can swim or canoe, and pavilions and water parks. Drop in at the Jurong Bird Park for an informal meeting with some 3,500 birds in the world's largest walk-in aviary and take in a show and have parrots talk to you. Yes, *talk* to you. It is a great thing to have parrots talk to you.

If the famed Zoological Gardens' attractions – that include petting snakes or sharing a cuppa with a friendly orangutan – are too passé for you, try the Night Safari, a cleverly assembled collection of assorted wildlife in their natural (simulated) habitat. A little train takes you through the jungles of the world, past a variety of wild animals. If you like shaking a leg, just walk the trails.

Haw Par Villa, also known as Tiger Balm Gardens, features a variety of weird and wonderful figures that re-create Chinese history and legends through grottos, tableaux and statues.

Located in the heart of town are the Botanical Gardens, from where the Brazilian rubber tree was distributed throughout Malaysia. I'm not much of a rubber tree fan, but definitely savoured the offerings of the café on the premises, that serves up a sumptuous breakfast.

As night falls, after-dark entertainment stirs to life. Numerous shows beckon. You could explore the harbourside and Chinatown before capping the evening with a drink at a downtown bar and a gourmet meal further down. Or cruise the waters of the busy port and have a buffet dinner aboard a Chinese junk. A sunset junk cruise around the scenic southern islands is a delightful – and very romantic – experience and affords a different view of the city's dramatic skyline.

Seeing me breakfasting alone one morning, one of the hotel managers asked if she could join me and we got chatting. You know how it is with hotel managers – they're always seeking chats with their guests in the hope of doing good networking and garnering more business or at the very least, imbibing more knowledge and tips on the industry and the marketplace. The lady was very pleasant, spoke well and had an easy smile. She told me that Singapore had a small but highly visible Sikh population and the local Sikhs were held in high esteem because of their entrepreneurial skills and fearless attitude. "Don't be surprised if you bump into one," she said with a smile as she left.

The city is totally walker-friendly, which suited me perfectly and so I started off on foot. The main boulevard,

Orchard Road, isn't just a mega shopping zone but is also window-shopper friendly, which also suited me well.

During my first three days, I must have traversed this hallowed, commercial strip of land some half a dozen times, in the process acquiring a pair of rather trendy brown shoes, a couple of T-shirts and a certain twang that was the hallmark of several shopkeepers with who I happened to chat. Having discovered a little sidewalk type café that dished out scalding hot coffee and absolutely delicious cheese cake, I would make it the starting and ending point of my daily forays. One by one, I did the rounds of the large department stores and designer-label boutiques that dot the road with territorial arrogance and got a fair idea of what brands of perfumes, goggles and pens were "in" and exactly how big a hole they drilled in one's pocket.

On one of my morning forays, while exiting a large department store on Orchard Road, I was accosted by a young Sikh gentleman who smilingly asked me if I was a visitor to the city and suggested a quick coffee if I had the time. As I had all the time in the world, I happily accepted. The fact is that I was becoming a bit weary of being all on my own all the time.

We walked into a little café which didn't serve cheese cake but had a wide assortment of other cakes, pastries and Chinese sweets and served the most delectable coffee imaginable. I lay great store in the quality of coffee I drink and it's one of the very few things about which I tend to get fussy about both at home and during my travels. The coffee there not only met, but surpassed my stringently high standards. It was hot and strong enough to hit the back of my tongue.

The gentleman's name was Sohinder, and he earned his livelihood by assisting his father in their family shipping business. Apparently, his family had been in this business for three generations and Singapore was the hub of their operations. Sohinder told me that, noticing a certain difficulty among the locals in pronouncing his name, he'd shortened it to Sohi, which, though not great, was infinitely better than Sonny or Sam, which were some of the other options. Sohi was closer to his roots. I agreed entirely with his reasoning. "Every Tom, Dick and Harry ends up being called Sam," I said with a serious expression on my face. Sohi seemed tickled to death with my response and actually pumped the air with his fist, the way you would do on hearing that you had been chosen to go into outer space or have dinner with Angelina Jolie or something as momentous as that.

Sohi proceeded to give me a rundown on his life. It turned out that he was born in Malaysia, had lived there for a while before moving to Singapore and had never been to India, though a visit was slated very soon. He was agog with excitement at the prospect and questioned me at length about the current social and economic trends in the country. I did my best in my role as a national spokesperson and gave him generous doses of culture, heritage and religion.

He asked if there were any Sikh movie stars in Bollywood and seemed a bit disappointed when I told him that as far as I knew there weren't any. Agreeing that India was a unique country, Indian food was the best in the world and that Bollywood actresses were gorgeously, we exchanged contact details and said goodbye.

The next day I changed track and made the pilgrimage to an institution I'd been hearing about for years. Singapore's Raffles Hotel, one of the world's premier 19th century hotels, is the brightest jewel in the city's crown and an upscale social rendezvous. Legendary symbol of all the fables of the exotic East, the Raffles reflects Singapore's history, ambience and cultural and social development.

Raffles became the embodiment of British colonial life in the tropics and it was here that the wealthy Malay rubber planters spent their money and leisure hours, seeking fun and excitement in the Long Bar, the Bar & Billiard Room and the Writers' Bar. The bars were also home to the Singapore Sling, first created by barman Ngiam Tong Boon in 1915. For one reason or the other, the hotel was always in the news and spawned numerous stories. One of the legends that made the rounds was about a tiger that was shot in 1902 under the billiards table, though the truth is that the animal was shot under the Bar & Billiard Room building which was built above ground.

Today, the Raffles welcomes guests in the grand style to which it has been accustomed for over a hundred years and I felt it appropriate to drop in. So what if I couldn't afford it. I had the time and the inclination and that's enough for an enterprising spirit like mine.

Rudyard Kipling once said "Feed at Raffles" and I intended to do just that. Armed with a little advice from the concierge, I lunched at the renowned Tiffin Room that specializes in traditional tiffin and Indian curries. As always, I believe I did fair justice to the meal, especially as it was spicy enough even for my unusual tastes. I had something that looked and tasted like mutton korma – it was sinfully delicious – accompanied by pilaf rice, green salad and yogurt. I was about to do similar justice to my coffee when I saw a Sikh couple seated at the other end of the restaurant. They smiled and waved at me and I smiled and waved back. That was their cue to come across and say hello, and they invited me to join them at their table. Partly out of politeness and partly because I didn't want my coffee to get cold, I gulped down my coffee with unusual alacrity and within some thirty seconds I was seated at their table. We got chatting. Like Sohi, they too instantaneously knew I was a visitor and introductions over, asked if there was anything they could do for me while I was in town. They could they show me the sights, if I hadn't seen them already or recommend restaurants and shopping outlets. Would I have time to have a drink with them sometime?

Thanking them, I told them I was doing fine and enjoying myself. They told me they were always happy to see another turbaned person around. There were far too few around as far as they were concerned, a sentiment I appreciated and shared. I knew exactly what they meant. I thanked them again, shook hands and we parted company.

The week had passed rather quickly and before I quite knew it, it was my last day in the city. Breaking my normal routine, I headed to Chinatown to buy something for my Mom, is was always reluctant to accept gifts but who, I knew, liked Chinese decorative pieces. Like most Chinatowns, Singapore's is normally bustling with activity and has exciting shopping options and outstanding Chinese cuisine and seafood.

But it was the eve of Chinese New Year and the place was relatively deserted and unusually quiet. Most of the shops had closed early. Finding one open but about to close, I barged in literally, as the owner was pulling the shutters down, inviting a huge glare. On my telling him I was a visitor to the city and wanted to buy a nice piece, he hesitated for a moment, then waved me in, with the glare still in place, saying, "Hurry, hurry, hurry!"

Well, it wasn't exactly the way I'd planned my shopping, but sizing up the situation, I hurried the way no other shopper probably ever had. Lest I hadn't got the message, my shopkeeper-friend hadn't moved away from the shutter and kept glancing at it for my benefit.

Giving everything on display a quick glance, I picked up a blue porcelain piece, which by coincidence matched the colour of my turban. "Good, good! Good choice, and good match," my shopkeeper-friend said, pointing to my turban. He was still glaring but seemed to have eased up a bit. While paying up, I wished him a happy new year. For the first time since our brief encounter, the frown on the old man's face was replaced by something that vaguely resembled a smile.

"Happy happy, same same!" he said. This time it *was* a smile.

Armed with my blue porcelain artefact, I left the good man's shop, barely managing to get my posterior out of the way as he pulled the shutter down with express speed and headed for a well-earned dinner before returning to my hotel.

All in all, it had been a fulfilling day in a city that is renowned for providing fulfilment in a variety of ways.

7

Jewels in the Forest

It's all about the fine art of good living.

Which, of course, is reason enough for an aficionado(self-proclaimed, admittedly) like me to stop by and give it a repeat visit.

Deep in the heart of Germany's Black Forest region, two exceptional hotels are going about their business with smooth efficiency, providing upscale clients unsurpassed comfort and luxury in sylvan surroundings. Recognized and ranked among Germany's top leisure hotels – they've swept national culinary and hospitality awards year after year – they go beyond normal standards to offer clients a special ambience built on pedigree, quality and privacy.

Hotel Traube Tonbach and Hotel Bareiss Im Schwarzwald personify top-end German and European elegance. At the same time they are simplicity itself. The combination can be a heady cocktail. Ask their privileged guests. Or just ask me – there's always me!

My visit to this scenic region got off to a great start, with an outing I'll cherish for long and for good reason.

Picture this scenario. Being driven around beautiful countryside is a rewarding enough experience by itself, but when your chauffeur happens to be a senior citizen and the car happens to be a vintage 1945 model Mercedes coupe on an Old Timer's Tour, it becomes an immensely more rewarding experience. It becomes a rare and special treat. And at 20 Euros per tour, it's almost a steal.

As we drove through patches of forest, along valleys and meadows and in and out of tiny villages, it was easy to understand why the Black Forest is one of Germany's main holiday regions. Throughout the drive, our guide-cum-chauffeur (who owns 11 vintage cars and drives just for a hobby, by the way), enlightened us about special features of the region. He told us about how important nature was to the locals and its impact on their lifestyles. And he told us about how times had changed, even here in the heart of rural Germany.

Indeed, the Black Forest region can be called the heart of rural Germany. Named after the tall coniferous trees which stretch for miles to form dark, dense forests, this is a special place —and for all the right reasons. Consider the value-enhancing attributes. A landscape that is the setting for one of Europe's most beautiful vacation spots, countless lookout points from where one can admire the scenic vistas, romantic valleys that harbour cheery little cafes and well-to-do farmsteads that welcome tourists with accommodation and home-cooked meals.

The brighter the sunshine, the darker the forests appear. And during summer and autumn, it is flower-power, incorporating all the colours of the rainbow, that is on display. Startlingly beautiful flowers hanging from windows and balconies greet the visitor at every turn. Winter sees the flowers replaced by ferns.

A great add-on to the tourist experience is the fact that here one can mingle freely and easily with locals and enjoy their simple-heartedness, seen everywhere from simple inns to prize-winning hotels. Playing host to vacationers are some eight communities located in natural settings, each community being unique in its own way. Their collective offering is among the region's great charms and nothing reflects this better than the regional festivals where locals don traditional jackets and traditional skirts called dirndls.

Nature's bounties notwithstanding, German preponderance with culture is evident here. Throughout the year there are concerts and traditional festivals. Some are trade-oriented, like the wine-festival for instance, where local produce is offered generously – It is best to be prudent here as the wine is stronger than you would imagine. Others provide sparkling entertainment, like the "Lighting of the Valley", which transforms the valley into a sea of firework displays and lit candles.

Food-wise, the hotels couldn't have been better located. While the whole of Germany offers quality food, the Black Forest region is a gourmet's delight. Traditional German food with a preponderance of pork and turkey, wholesome desserts of ice creams and the famous Black Forest cakes, is complemented by nouvelle cuisine, a happy combination that has landed local restaurants half a dozen Michelin stars. And at least three local chefs who have been associated with the hotel at some point in their careers, have celebrity status. Harald Wohlfahrt, Claus-Peter Lumpp and Jorg Sackmann are household names for people who make food their business, or their pleasure.

Functioning from three buildings, Hotel Traube Tonbach welcomes guests to its special world. As many as twenty-one different room categories, stretching from small single rooms to the 200 sq. metre Romantik-Suite, make you feel at home in the midst of period furniture. There's this ambience around that you get pretty used to pretty quickly.

Shortly after I'd checked-in, I bumped into an American lady who was also a guest at the hotel. I was doing the rounds of the premises it seemed so was she. The only difference was that I was trying to look around with a professional journalistic view, while she was doing it just as something you do now and then. I first saw her on the verandah that takes in generous amounts of sunshine and offers wonderful views of pine forests and meadows, a hallmark of the Black Forest region. I ran into her again at the outdoor swimming pool, which coincidentally, also offers pristine views of the countryside.

The smile she flashed at me had a sweetness to it which stuck a rather favourable chord in me. Keen to return the compliment, I flashed her back my own version of a supposedly sweet smile – the very best in my repertoire. Pleasantries exchanged, we found ourselves chatting in the sun. Her name was Katie, she was in the fashion business and operated a chain of small, exclusive boutiques in America. She was holidaying in Germany and this was her first visit to the Black Forest region. I told her what I did to stay honest, gave her a brief rundown on my life and we parted company after what I thought – rather delightfully, I must admit – was a rather affectionate handshake. It might have been just my fevered imagination, but I sensed she fancied me. You know that certain instinctive feeling men of the world get from time to time. Yes, sir, I could sense it.

But plagued with the thought of several women having fancied me and all of it leading to nothing, I resigned myself to my fate, dismissed her from my mind and carried on with my hotel investigation tour.

Cuisine is a strong point of the hotel and it has four totally diverse restaurants in the establishment. In the three-star gourmet restaurant Schwarzwaldstube, where they change the menu every two months, guests get to enjoy the culinary art of renowned chefs. In the Silberberg, your palate is tempted with a fresh daily menu. And as guests in the Kohlerstube and Bauernstube, you'll be spoilt for choice. From light, international gourmet cuisine, to Swabian delicacies and the regional specialities of the Black Forest, it is all high feasting – adventurous, bold, and epicurean.

Having savoured a wonderful lunch at Schwarzwaldstube, I followed some of the enlightened - looking guests, and ended up at the coffee terrace. Incidentally this is essentially the place for crisp bread rolls and fresh juices among blooming rosebuds. And afternoons are the domain of the master confectioner, whose cakes, pastries, flans and gateaux are nationally famous.

"Hi. Mind if I join you?" I hadn't noticed Katie come up, but there she was, standing tall before me. I did notice now that she looked very pretty. Very pretty indeed! She'd changed into a very trendy outfit that did her credit and seemed in a relaxed, chatty mood. We chatted the way strangers who've met up on a holiday chat and finally started to open up and divulged a bit about our lives to each other. As often happens when I'm talking to foreigners, the topic shifted to Sikhism and Katie asked if I'd mind telling her something about the religion and what it stood for. All full of charm, I told her I didn't mind at all, and told her whatever I could in a capsule form, providing a brief induction. Sort of like a brief resume designed for quick education.

While we were talking, I found that I couldn't keep my eyes off her, which made an uneasy feeling gnaw at me. I was a bit annoyed at my apparent lack of self-control, and the amazing speed with which I was growing fond of the girl. It unnerved me, to say the least. I was dying to ask her if she was expecting to meet someone that evening, but obviously didn't want to appear silly, or rude, or forward, or whatever I would have appeared if I'd asked and so didn't. I just tried hard to keep my mind off her and on other things. I still don't know how or why it happened, but after what I can only describe as a very pleasant little meeting, things just somehow wound to a halt and we abruptly parted company. It just happened. One moment we were chatting, and the next she'd said goodbye and was gone. And that was that.

The next day I moved out and checked in at Hotel Bareiss Im Schwarzwald, for what turned out to be a continuation of the good life. "Forget your waistlines," said the team of forty-three chefs. And most guests obliged. Well, I certainly did! I'm like that. Always a good sport who gets into the spirit of things, no matter what, especially when it pertains to spirits and food.

As is my wont, I set out to explore the hotel. A typical day here starts with the Bareiss breakfast presented as a large buffet in the lobby, with everything from croissants and cakes to cold meat and shrimp cocktails, and sekt (German champagne). The Dorfstuben is where guests gather for freshly-drawn pils and snacks. And in fine weather, light summer dishes can be enjoyed in the pool restaurant Oase, which sports an easy ambience.

Inspired by French-Mediterranean cooking, the restaurant Bareiss features among Germany's ten best gourmet places. The chef, Claus Peter Lumpp was an institution by himself, and providing that extra touch was a wine menu featuring seven hundred choices and a festive, elegant environment.

Providing pleasurable encounters with classical European cuisine and favourites like lamb carre au gratin, red barbell filet on a lemon grass sauce, or penne in parmesan is the Kaminstube menu. There is a choice of wines from Alsace, Baden or Wurttemberg. In summer you're served on the lovely terrace, while in winter you sit by an open fire.

"Hi. Mind if I join you?" I froze with surprise – the same words from the same person! It my dear friend Katie, looking resplendent in a trendy outfit, perhaps even trendier than the one she wore the previous afternoon. "Where did you disappear? I asked for you at the reception and they told me you'd checked out and moved here. You didn't mention it to me. I had no idea you were set to do that." She seemed a bit petulant, bit on her upper lip as if in deep thought and then flashed me a huge smile that lit up her face – and everything around as well. I mumbled something which sounded like half an explanation, half an apology. It was apparent to me now that I'd blundered big time. Instead of trying to spend time with the gorgeous lady, I'd not only not tried to renew contact with her, but had actually left the hotel without saying goodbye.

I don't know what had come over me. I hadn't meant to be rude. I guess my mind was wandering around and I just wasn't focused enough on her. Deep down, I think I had a certain sense of resignation and was convinced nothing would come out of this chance meeting and liaison. So she'd slipped out of my mind. Providentially, she'd sought me out again and actually come over to meet me. Armed with a great urge to kick myself, I just smiled instead and did my best at damage control, while thanking my stars for this great revival of my rather modest and mundane fortunes.

I honestly don't know what made me say it, but I told her that I was deliberately avoiding her because she'd moved me more than she should have, considering we'd met just twice, and that too relatively briefly. I wasn't lying. In fact I wasn't even thinking when I just blurted it out. That was it! The die was cast. Now there was this awkward silence that lasted some five or six seconds and then she sort of whispered "How sweet. How very sweet of you to say that. Gee, that's just the kind of thing a woman wants to hear, out on holiday in a lovely place like this. You know what. You're a sweetie." And she leaned across and planted two huge kisses on my cheeks.

I'm not even going to try to describe how I felt at that moment or what my heartbeat rate was. I think it was at least two thousand per minute, but I could be wrong. The Bareiss arcade, where we had met, is an absolutely wonderful place for browsing and shopping for choice wines, cosmetics, fashion items, exclusive textiles, jewellery and precious stones. But right then, at that particular moment, nothing shone as brightly as this gorgeous woman who'd waltzed into my life literally out of the blue. You could call it a bolt from the blue in the Black Forest.

Somewhat giddy-headed, I invited Katie for a drink and she accepted my offer with a huge smile and something that sounded like, "Oh, with pleasure," or something like that. Or maybe she'd said "leisure". Or "treasure". Or something similar. The truth is that I wasn't thinking straight or hearing right. I was still in a shock at the fact that a beautiful woman of the world had followed me from one wonderful hotel to another and was actually propositioning me.

In Forster-Jacob-Stuble and the Uhrenstuble, both authentic Black Forest 19th century ploughman's bars, you are served hearty hot-and-cold Black Forest specialities, like home-made style sausages and bacon, smoked schaufele (smoked pork loin) and bread from a wood oven. Accompanied perhaps with a regional wine, a good Kirsch or local draught pils. Forming the backdrop for over 20,000 bottles in the wine cellar, are a selection of old French menus, historic wine-growing implements and the history of the corkscrew. If I hadn't met Katie I'd have probably gone deep into the history of the corkscrew, but right now I had better things to do.

Katie and I lingered over our drinks and the white wine went down very smoothly indeed. We talked and talked and I felt myself drawn to this lovely looking woman with her lovely sense of dress. I vaguely recall telling myself that all this was too good to be true, and the mirage would disappear soon. But this was no mirage, and no fantasy bubble. Just heaven on earth.

Like everything sublime, it had to end. Katie told me she had to leave as she was expecting a friend who was driving from Frankfurt just to see her. She had a lovely look on her face and I couldn't help feeling a little pang. I don't know exactly what it was. It wasn't exactly jealousy, but I have to admit it was something like a feeling of emptiness. I felt a sense of despair and that in turn made me desperate. I don't know if I appeared despairing or desperate, or both. I guess my face was an open book because Katie leaned over to me and whispered in my ear. "Oh, it isn't anything like that. It's just someone with who I went to college in the States." She smiled and planted another deadly kiss on my cheek. Feeling utterly foolish, I gave her a huge hug and kiss and tried to look nonchalant about the whole thing, disguising the fact that I wanted to kick myself. I came out to the porch to see her off, gave her another kiss as she got into the cab and then went up to my room to sit back and think myriad noble thoughts.

The fact is that I wasn't thinking clearly. I desperately needed a diversion to get this woman out of my mind. She'd stamped her personality on my entire thought process and was riding roughshod on my mind without meaning to. That's how serious this whole business had become in such a short span of time. Or maybe, while I hated admitting it to myself, the truth was that that's how vulnerable and exposed I really was. The thought troubled me immensely.

All in all, it had been a delightful interlude. I'd enjoyed the extraordinary hospitality levels offered by both Hotel Traube Tonbach and Hotel Bareiss Im Schwarzwald, both exceptional hotels. And the icing on the cake was the company of a vivacious, friendly lady who'd conveyed her liking for me. It was more than what a mere mortal could ask for. Along my sense of elation was a feeling of foreboding, I don't know why.

We exchanged goodbyes on the phone later that night, told each other how much we'd enjoyed each other's company and bade each other well. To my credit, my voice sounded almost normal, though the truth is I felt anything but that.

Katie and I kept in touch and I caught up with her six months later. Over a leisurely lunch at a downtown New York bistro, we brought each other abreast with our news. Inevitably, the conversation shifted to our brief trysts in the beautiful Black Forest region and the wonderful moments we'd spent together in two outstanding hotels. Suddenly, and totally out of context, she asked me exactly how I'd felt when she'd said she had to leave to be with her friend. "Were you jealous?" she asked.

She had this rather serious expression and was staring keenly at my face. I wasn't expecting it and my face must have betrayed my surprise. "Were you jealous? Did you feel any sort of jealousy? You don't have to answer this if you don't want to. It's just that I'd like to know. I guess I *need* to know." She was smiling now, but I could see that she was absolutely serious. Strangely, she also looked a bit nervous.

I was on thin ice. This wasn't the first time a woman had asked me if I'd felt jealous while with them, but this time it was harder, simply because I knew I hadn't been jealous. And yet my face had conveyed some such emotion. I took a deep breath and told her I hadn't felt any jealousy, just a feeling of total emptiness. "So the thought of my leaving made you lonely?" She was looking at me intently. "Yes it did. It not only made me feel lonely right then at that particular time, but with my entire existence. I felt lonely as hell," I said. Glad to get that off my chest, I gave her an affectionate hug and sought, and got, my customary kiss on the cheek.

Keen to step off the thin ice, I delved into small talk and told her I had a whacky idea. How about my partnering her in her business and opening a boutique in Delhi? That way I could spend my old age selling women's fashion clothing and accessories. She flashed me a huge smile and gave a strange look. "Oh, how strange that you should say that, because I had actually meant to ask you what you thought about the idea of my stocking and selling turbans in America. They look so beautiful and dignified, I'm sure they'll be a big hit. And of course, you could model them exclusively for me. How's that for something to consider, mister?" I told her it was a terrific idea. She smiled and leaned closer to me and whispered in my ear. "But I don't want to wait around till I get old. I'd rather sell them now, while I'm young and beautiful enough to arouse strong passions in turbaned men."

She kissed me again and this time the kiss wasn't just deadly. It was far more lethal than that. But experience counts! Having been kissed so often by her, I was now a man of the world, so to say. Which meant that my heartbeat wasn't two thousand per minute.

It was much, much more!

8

Two Days in Chitwan

You know how it is. When people get tired, they tend to become edgy and testy. That's just what was happening. Just about everyone in the van was getting a bit impatient.

We'd left Pokhara early in the morning to catch memorable glimpses of the mountains getting the day's first touch of sunshine. We had hurried through breakfast, tumbled into the van and left the hotel without fuss or ceremony. And yet, six hours later, we were still on the highway, a bit tired, dusty and very thirsty.

Not that there was traffic or breakdown or anything like that. It just took a long time to negotiate all those curves on the road and the hurried tea-stops we'd made twice didn't help.

At last, we made reached our destination. The scorching sun notwithstanding, the mood lifted and the smiles came back. The long ride was behind us and the bounties of nature and wilderness lay ahead.

The Royal Chitwan National Park is a majestic, downright primeval area of wilderness, teeming with wildlife.

Bird calls fill the air. At certain spots the foliage is so lush you need to force your way through. Vast seas of elephant grass ripple beneath you as you move around and everywhere there's silence and a pervading sense of relaxation.

The drive to our lodgings, Tiger Tops tented camp, located some forty kilometres from Sauruha, gave us the perfect insight into Chitwan's nature and terrain.

The camp turned out to be a delight, offering just the right amount of luxury amid the wilderness. The first impression we got was that we were indeed in the midst of wild animals in their natural habitat.

Awaiting us was the manager, who said he needed to talk to us. He'd obviously rehearsed this speech dozens, if not hundreds of times and started off immediately.

"Welcome to the camp. I hope you'll enjoy the experience. Just keep two things in mind – don't extinguish the little lamps that are placed outside your tents and don't walk out of the camp area at night. Other than that, you don't have to worry about anything. You'll be safe here." Everyone was suitable impressed. "There's this question of rhinos, you see," the good man continued, with the seriousness such a statement deserved. "Rhinos are very dangerous animals and sometimes they tend to sneak right up to our camp."

Needless to say, we didn't extinguish the little lamps that dangled outside our tents like shiny markers and we certainly didn't venture out of the camp area during the night.

For those interested in being far from the crowds and for those who cherish a genuine wilderness experience, Chitwan is just what is required. The park is one of the rare surviving examples of the continuous stretch of forest and grassland that once spanned the area between the Indus river, right up to the Myanmar border. Some 70 per cent of the park comprises sal-forested hills that harbour a varied and rich wildlife. The best-known areas are the flat floodplains of the three rivers that bound the park – the Reu, Rapti and Narayani. This is a region of grasslands, criss-crossed by meandering streams and dotted with marshes, swamps and lakes.

About a fifth of the park is savannah, with over fifty different species of grasses forming a carpet. Along the water courses lie the river-fed forests of shisham and khair, while further inland are kapok trees. And then, of course, there are the sal trees which tower above everything.

Chitwan's wildlife includes over forty species of mammals, including wild boar, sambar deer, spotted deer, buffalo, leopard, sloth bear, one-horned rhino and the ever eagerly sought-after—the Royal Bengal Tiger.

The game-stalking and viewing can be done by jeep, on foot, by dugout canoe or on elephant back. This is in fact one of the few wilderness parks in the world that allows visitors to roam around on foot. But believe me, it isn't something you want to overdo, especially if you aren't accompanied by a trained ranger guide.

And that's just what I did. Within an hour of arriving at the camp, I was out walking the jungle with a small group of visitors led by a guide named Biswal. Just a few short steps got us to a clearing where a herd of deer were grazing. They seemed oblivious to our presence. So were the other animals we saw, which to me simply meant that perhaps there were too many visitors thronging these parts of the park.

It was while lunching in the open that we were told about the elephant ride. It sounded like a terrific idea and an hour later, there I was, perched on an elephant that seemed just a little jumpy, scouring the jungle for wildlife sightings. If it was excitement I was seeking, I found it in abundance. And it took a mere few seconds to unfold.

We spotted a rhino about a hundred metres away and our group of three elephants set about flanking it. "It's dangerous," I told the mahout. "We're getting too close and cornering him. I don't think that's a good idea." But he just smiled and nodded. I didn't like what was happening. The elephants were closing in on the cantering rhino and we could see he'd have to stop because there was a twenty-foot drop just ahead of him. Stop he did, and then turned right onto us. When rhinos charge, even elephants react and our worthy animal saved the day with an elegant side-step and backtrack that just about averted a collision. Talk about close shaves!

This certainly wiped the smile off our mahout's face. "You were quite right, sir," he said to me a bit sheepishly. In my grand, inimitable style, I just patted him on the shoulders as if to say, "It's all right."

My two-day stay at Chitwan had provided a fulfilling experience in every sense of the word. More than the wildlife sightings, it was the mere fact of being in the wild that was charming.

And with word of our elephant ride having spread, everyone from every group in the camp came up to me at the bonfire dinner to compliment me on my foresight and jungle sense.

Of course, out of a sense of being a good sport, I didn't reveal the fact that this had been my first elephant ride in the wild and that I didn't have a clue about how rhinos behaved.

Everyone around thought I was a seasoned jungle hand and it wouldn't have been fair to have spoilt their fun. Especially as there were some pretty ladies among them who were beginning to take a little more than general interest in me.

9

Gstaad Gasps

The crisp early morning sunshine lit up the Lac Leman and the town of Montreaux that adjoins it. But I was in Montreaux just to board the famous train MOB Express to the scenic Gstaad, undertaking what everyone had been telling me would be a memorable journey.

For sure, the journey on the MOB Express was memorable, thanks to the picturesque scenery. Mountains and green meadows passed us by as we glided along the foot of mountains and we could actually feel the spray from waterfalls that resembled silver streaks. A couple of hours of bliss and we arrived at the end of our journey.

Located in the Swiss mountain region of Saanenland, Gstaad is arguably one of the world's most upscale and renowned resorts. Gstaad is famous for its ski slopes, sunshine, and billionaires. Everyone had said the resort was somewhat "snooty and special" and everyone was somewhat right. I wasn't disappointed.

Legend has it that when God created the Saanenland, He pressed His hand firmly against the earth. The print of His palm is where the villages of Saanen and Gstaad stand today. The little finger formed the Kalberhoni, the ring finger cut out the valley for the commune of Gsteig, the middle finger was responsible for the Lauenen Valley, the index finger for the Turbach Valley and the thumb smoothed the ground for Schonried and Saanenmoser.

Gstaad welcomed me rather quietly. The train station is small and in a matter of minutes I was in my hotel just across the street, gradually starting to observe my surroundings in detail. The landscape is superb, the climate mild, and there is hardly any fog in the Gstaad Super Ski Pass with 250 km of downhill runs or in the walking and hiking trails that have made it world-famous and the host of several major international events.

Situated between 1,000 and 3,000 metres above sea level in the western part of the Bernese Oberland, at the confluence of the Valaisan, Vaudois and the Bernese Alps, the Saanenland is nature's paradise. While Gstaad is the tourist centre, each of the small towns offer something different to visitors. The medieval village of Saanen with its historic dwellings that lies in the shadow of the splendid Church of St. Maurice, is the seat of the local administration, Schonried is a sunny terrace high above the River Saane, Saanenmoser is the departure point for exciting walking tours, Gsteig-Feutersoey is a picturesque mountain village and Lauenen is untouched Alpine country at its best.

A wide valley and gentle slopes ensure generous sunshine for the Saanenland, giving it the nickname Sonnenland or sun country and this explains why the region was popular for relaxation even in the 17th century. Tourism in this region has always enjoyed an ongoing boom through history. It was greatly boosted by the opening, in 1905, of the Montreaux-Oberland Railway (MOB), which provided a direct scenic link between Montreaux (on Lake Geneva) and Zweisinnen. A further boost came by way of the 1920 opening of the Institute Le Rosey and also the Gstaad Palace. Having spent their teens in Gstaad, many former Rosey students from privileged families retained a lifelong attachment for the region.

The Saanenland holiday, with Gstaad as the base, gives an opportunity to indulge in the excellent and varied sports available in the region. Walk along narrow trails that snake across the mountains, climb, mountain-bike, para glide, go ballooning, white-water rafting or canoeing, play golf or tennis in summer – the choices are endless. Come winter and the activity revolves around downhill and cross-country skiing, ski touring, snowboarding, ice skating and tobogganing. Winters are high season in the Gstaad Super Ski Region. Ski enthusiasts from the world over indulge themselves with some 250 km of downhill ski runs, 69 cable cars and ski lifts, 100 km of cross-country trails, 40 km of skating and curling rinks, reputed downhill and cross-country ski schools and cosy mountain restaurants with sunny terraces.

Small but immensely classy, that's Gstaad for the visitor. Its main road is also its main shopping and office centre, neatly bisecting the town. You can walk its length in ten minutes or two hours, depending on your priorities. This is where the world's billionaires come to shop for exclusive designer labels in clothes and ski equipment. A charming touch is added by hotels and houses, all constructed in the Saanen style, in harmony with the surrounding countryside. Keeping a steadfast vigil over the town from its vantage point is the Grand Hotel whose famous doors have routinely opened for world leaders and celebrities.

Old trades like scissors-cutting, pottery, wood-carving, and alphorn-making are still in vogue. The farmers earn their living from cattle breeding and dairy farming and are intensely proud of their Saanen-Hobalkase (local cheese). In spring and autumn, you can watch the traditional festive cattle ascent or descent from the high pastures, with the farmers sporting traditional costumes and the cattle adorned with flowers.

Sipping hot coffee at a café just off the main boulevard, I could see people browsing around the shops, the tourists among them identifiable due to their cameras. Very few cars disturb the peace of the town, and about the only time there was a flurry of movement was when a train pulled up at the station. The Alps form a ring around the town and in the distance you could see brightly coloured hang gliders moving like dragonflies across the mountainous terrain.

Whether you choose to have breakfast on the Alps, or a candlelit dinner in a mountain hut, or do a snow-shoe hike, or anything else that is crazy or zany enough, chances are that you are doing it in the company of the world's rich and famous, for it is mainly they who like to frequent this famous mountain resort.

I can vouch for the fact that I was perhaps the only ordinary person present in the town during my visit and stay. But then, I've always prided myself on my splendid exclusivity and this was very true here.

10

Khantoke and Softness

Khantoke and softness — that's the best way to describe it.

One pleasant summer evening in Chiang Mai, I ended up at one of the city's upscale restaurants famed for its Thai food-cum-cultural evenings. Dinners accompanied by cultural shows are very popular all over Thailand and Chiang Mai offers some of the finest. They make quite a big deal out of all this but with good reason. These occasions give you a chance to enjoy the traditional Thai way of life and some excellent food — the food in Northern Thailand is different from what you find in the rest of the country. On all my visits, I've looked forward to these evenings, but then history records that I look forward to most things that are related to good food.

Seeing and absorbing Chiang Mai's special charm and attractions, the day had gone by rather pleasantly. Old folklore says the city emerged from the mists. You can make what you like of this, but the fact is that Chiang Mai's combination of natural beauty and kind people with their social graces gives it a paradise type character that fills your entire being with peace and happiness.

Nestling at the foot of forested mountains, Thailand's second largest city after Bangkok is at its heart a large village, famed for its attractive features like misty mountain scenery, 14th century historical temples, fruit and flower cultivation, an assortment of handicrafts, and courteous locals. Some five centuries ago, Chiang Mai was the proud capital of Lan Na Thai – the kingdom of one million rice fields – the first independent Thai kingdom in the fabled Golden Triangle. Prolonged prosperity elevated the city to great prominence in religion, culture and trade, right until its sacking and reduction to a vassal state by a Burmese invasion in 1556. When the Burmese were expelled in 1775, Lan Na Thai re-joined the mainstream of Northern Thailand. Today, the city is on the ascendancy graph, thriving on a flourishing tourism influx, an elaborate handicrafts industry, superb natural surroundings and fertile orchards.

I had the privilege of visiting Wat Phra That Doi Suthep, the city's most important temple. Majestically perched on a hilltop overlooking the city, with priceless Buddhist relics stored in its 16th century golden pagoda and offering fabulous views, the temple provides a soothing experience to the visitors.

I said a short prayer, walked around the complex, was blessed by an attendee monk and left feeling calmed and composed, the way you do when you have visited a holy place.

I also managed to spend time browsing and admiring local handicrafts at bustling roadside markets. With the city being Thailand's main handicraft centre with numerous local cottage-industries that boast skilled craftsmanship in fabrics, silk and wood carving, shopping is a great local adventure. While shops have sprung up all over the city, the shopping hotspot is the renowned Bo Sang San

Kamphaeng Road area where you can also see artisans at work. The Night Bazaar is the place for anything from everyday clothes to fancy music systems – and some robust bargaining. An extraordinary range of items from antiques to silver jewellery, lacquerware and silks, line the noisy bazaars, making shoppers spoilt for choice.

And now here I was, dutifully seated in the restaurant, looking forward to the evening and the meal. The place was packed with tourists, the waiters scurried around with the orders and different troupes were performing on the stage. Just as I was settling down in anticipation of enjoying my khantoke meal – one of my long-time favourites – as many as three pretty ladies came up to me, seemingly appearing from nowhere. Thai women have this knack of appearing out of nowhere. I think it is because they're slim and dainty. Anyway, there they were. It was a gentle, welcome intrusion into my culinary delights.

A speciality meal of Northern Thailand, Khantoke is a real treat, especially for gourmets who enjoy distinct flavours and textures in their food. You sit at low tables, slide your feet under them and the food is brought and served to you with some fanfare. With a few exceptions, a typical Khantoke meal comprises a large platter with little bowls of assorted items – chicken, pork, lamb, vegetables and salads, all eaten with sticky rice called lah.

In my opinion, this type of cuisine is serious business and deserves undivided attention. So I can be excused for not noticing the ladies immediately. They just waited till they'd got my attention, smiled and then escorted me gently on to the stage. It was as simple as that. The other guests seemed quite happy at my presence on the stage and some clapped, some smiled and some nodded their heads.

The next five minutes saw me turn a performer. I was showered with rose petals and politely cajoled into joining the dance. With a grace I didn't know I possessed, I copied the girls' actions with precision and went through the elaborate, soft movements of an Oriental harvest dance. I don't quite know how I managed it, but I seemed to blend in rather nicely. The dance sequence done, I was courteously led back to my table.

Not a word was spoken and there was no fuss or ceremony involved during this little affair. But there was no shortage of applause. I'd like to think that some among the audience actually admired my dancing. I'll never know if they did, but just about everyone in the restaurant seemed to be happy at the sight of a Sikh trying his hand – or should I say hands and feet – at his version of a Northern Thai harvest dance.

The ambience was classy, the dancers exceedingly pretty and the Khantoke meal was as good as any I've tasted in the "country of smiles".

Not exactly overburdened with modesty, I thought it totally appropriate and fair to narrate this particular incident to all and sundry wherever and whenever I could find them. And so, one fine evening, while dining with a lady friend, I gave a rather detailed blow-by-blow account of my celebrated evening in Chiang Mai.

Convinced that my friend had been duly impressed and charmed, I puffed my chest out and sort of waited for her reaction. After all, such great things don't happen too often and certainly not to all people.

After what seemed like an eternity, she did react. With a straight face she said she envied me and was sure this particular episode cum adventure would stand me in good stead. Flashing me a huge smile, added, "Well, now that you've had this wonderful experience in Thailand, I'm sure your fortunes will soar," she said softly. "What I mean is that if you just assert yourself less and dance to women's tunes more often, your life in this department will certainly look up."

11

The Turbaned Groom

The turbaned groom – well, sort of.

The night was young, the place charming and there was a pleasant buzz in my head.

That made it three good reasons for me to jive and I've been known to do just that on scores of occasions for much less. Szeged has many attributes and one of them is that it can truly be called the "heart" of Hungary. The city has a rich history, and there's plenty you can do here. History beckons at all corners and heritage monuments await you at every turn.

Situated at the mouth of the Maros and on both sides of the Tisza, Szeged is a town that boasts of some substance and has to be taken seriously. It is south-east Hungary's third largest provincial town, its economic, administrative and cultural centre and the seat of Csongrad County. These attributes apart, it also serves the tastiest soups money can buy.

Mine was a quiet entry to the city at night. A typical late-night check-in, hasty dinner and a good night's sleep was about all the excitement on day one. But tomorrow was another day, I told myself. I was tired and sleep came easily.

And quite a day "tomorrow" turned out to be. When I woke up, there was morning glory to be savoured. Birds chirped on branches that brushed my room's balcony and soft sunlight filtered in through lace curtains. The strong smell of coffee and a stronger urge to get out and explore the city eased me into an action-mode.

The region carries the burden of a rich and eventful history. In the 2nd century, Szeged was a Roman outpost; in the 5th century it was Attila the Hun's seat; in the 9th century the conquering Magyar Chiefs held their first national assembly in the present-day Opusztaszer; and the 11th century saw the settlement become part of the royal estate. And 1728 was the year of the infamous witchcraft trials with thirteen people burnt on the stake – the peninsula of the Tisza bank where this happened is still called Boszorkany (witch) Island. In 1849 the town was briefly the national capital. Today, the town has become a city that thrives on tourism and commerce.

My sightseeing tour started at the city's true icon. Set along the lines of the bridge in Venice and made in honour of Franz Joseph, Emperor of Austria and King of Hungary (1848–1916), the Bridge of Sighs is a unique monument. Walking along cobbled streets, I headed for the downtown area that's literally bursting with architectural standouts and cultural and art treasures.

Built as a park with artistic statues – the buildings lining it giving it a unifying effect – Szechenyiter must surely rank among Hungary's most beautiful squares. Close by stands the Town Hall, a grand old building with an impressive facade that shows great artistic taste, fluting a harmony of styles.

Awaiting your leisure is the neo-classic style Grunn Orban House that features Hungary's first printing house and the famous balcony decorated with the "Attila relief". Pictures, statues, period furniture and pharmacy exhibits greet you in the Palace of Culture, a museum strong on its depiction of local history. From there I moved on to the neo-classic Zsoter House, a former military hospital and later a national government building and ended up at the Votive Church, Hungary's fourth largest church.

Statues to the right of me, statues to the left of me – it is like a flood. The city seems to have been overrun by statues. They come thick-and-fast and seem to be everywhere. There are statues of famous personalities like Ferenc Rokoczi, Ferenc Deak, Lajos Kossuth, Pal Vasarhelyi, Istvan Szechenyi and Lajos Tisza. And in the pool in front of the Town Hall, rest the symbolic brown "Blessed and Destructive Tisza Statues".

You see another face of the city on the left embankment of the Tisza. Renowned for its houses surrounded by gardens, sports grounds and open-air baths, and broad parks Ujszeged provides a breath of fresh air to the visitor. The Botanical Garden with its ornamental park with glass and foil houses, the rock and rose garden and ponds provide for a pleasant experience.

A really smart thing to do here is to invest some time and effort to take the local cuisine seriously, and shedding your controls. I mean that. If succumbing to hunger was ever a pleasure, it is here. Like most things Hungarian, the cuisine too has its source in strong traditions. They're strong on meats. A classic example is the Szeged salami, also called winter salami. The heat once destroyed the salami's mould, so its production was limited to winter, hence the name. The secret of the seasonings was handed down from generation to generation of butchers, with the salami-master being the only one to know the proportions of ground spices to be mixed with the minced meat.

As for Hungarian paprika, it's an institution in its own right as the entire world knows. Step out into the countryside and at every turn you're greeted by fiery red garlands suspended from ceilings. It's these little devils that form the base of the famed paprika.

Spicy salami goes down rather easily with the light table wines of the sandy vineyards, produced in the sunny region between the Tisza and the Danube and also with Csongrad's red wine and Pusztamerges' Riesling. The local claim to fame, however, and the signature dish, is the celebrated Szeged fish head soup, a top-notch local delicacy prepared and served with much fanfare and not to be missed for love or money.

While enjoying this delectable dish one evening at a restaurant famed for its traditional cuisine, I found myself literally hustled to the stage, along with two other gentlemen from our group. Having spent a couple of days in Budapest and then a couple more discovering the charms of the Puszta – the Hungarian Great Plain – I'd got somewhat used to the plum and apricot brandies they'd been offering wherever we'd been and I must say they were going down very nicely indeed. My sense of refinement prevented me from refusing any drinks offered to me with love and so all I can say is that I'd drunk rather not wisely, but too well. All primed up, I was looking forward to an evening of mirth and merriment.

Well, mirth and merriment came soon enough. Before we could say "Szeged beloved" the three of us had been patted on the back vigorously, draped with traditional

Hungarian robes, garlanded, patted enthusiastically on the back again and literally pitch-forked into a robust dance. And I actually mean robust dance. Dancing has never been my strong point, but I manfully shrugged off my feeling of hesitation and plunged in. I'd never imagined myself possessing such energy levels, but if ever an occasion demanded high-voltage energy, this was it. It was literally a wild flurry of movements out there and I remember telling myself it was a miracle the stage didn't collapse.

Then came a wedding ceremony that, in effect, "married us off" in traditional local style to three girls who by chance or design, looked suitably demure but pretty as anything. They were all wearing similar, highly colourful costumes that did them great credit and they all had long hair that came down to their hips. There was a set pattern to the proceedings. We bowed to our "brides", and they bowed to us. They flashed us shy smiles and we tried to do the same. We then exchanged garlands and kisses, clasped their hands in ours, bowed again and then proceeded to dance with them. If the previous dance had been robust, this one was super-exuberant. The next five minutes featured a frenzy of action. Arms and legs flayed around, creating one big blur of movement. Everything was spinning in my head.

We were then ceremoniously escorted off the stage by our brides, kissed goodbye and the event became a part of memory. Somewhere along the way, I'd sort of felt that the girls were being a bit partial to me. You know how it is when you notice little things and over-read their meaning. "They fancy me, of course," I told myself smugly and then dismissed the thought from my mind, remembering the numerous occasions where I'd harboured such notions without any tangible results.

But for once, I'd got it right. Our tour leader later told me that I should feel privileged and flattered as the three girls had tossed a coin to decide who would have the privilege of being the bride of the guest with the turban. Well, I did feel flattered and privileged.

The rest of the evening was equally wonderful. The famed fish head soup, was sinfully delicious and worthy of all the praise heaped on it. They let us keep the robes as souvenirs, and as for the girls, all I can say is that they were pretty enough to make us smuggle them out of the country.

The fact that I didn't do that bears testimony to the fact that I've spent my entire professional life just being a serious travel journalist with a serious bent of mind, all those plum and apricot brandies, notwithstanding.

12

The Hague

Once, on my asking a group of young Dutch tourists I had met to describe their cities, they termed Amsterdam as "fun and leisure-oriented", Rotterdam as "more serious" and The Hague as "also there of course". You might say diplomats and bureaucrats rubbing shoulders doesn't really promise anything more. Or does it?

My belief is that The Hague can surprise you in more ways than one. With its exciting though subdued nightlife, its wide-open spaces and easy ambience and all its attractions that are so easy to access, it is definitely a place to visit.

Small it may be, but the city is undeniably of national importance. It is the home to the Queen of the Netherlands and the seat of its government. It is also the permanent headquarters of the International Court of Justice. If we add national governance and all those resident foreign embassies and missions, it makes quite a package.

Sure, there are no great crowds to talk about, no bustling cafes as we know them and no carnivals around. But then the cafes and pubs aren't empty either. In fact they are mostly full, with an international clientele meeting and relaxing over a coffee or a drink at the friendly downtown pub.

Dubbed the aristocrat of Dutch cities, The Hague is spread out, green and leafy. And the sea is close enough to lend its salty flavours and freshness to the air. Old buildings, wide tree-lined boulevards abound, and almost every corner sports parks and gardens. You find an interesting urban mix of new architecture and older monuments in the city.

Your city discovery tour could start at the enormously proportioned Binnenhof that is the centre of political life. Its large medieval hall, formerly used for state occasions, is now embraced and influenced by the daring modern curves of the Tweede Kamer, the Netherlands's celebrated House of Commons.

The grand structure contains other grand structures within its confines, like the 13th century Knights' Hall, which glitters with stained glass windows and pretty tapestries. It is worthwhile touring the Knights' Hall and the adjacent Parliament buildings. And it is worthwhile continuing on, to admire one of Rembrandt's finest self-portraits displayed proudly in the Mauritshuis Museum. Equally worthwhile and worthy of a visit is the Dr. Anton Philipszaal which features performances by the Netherlands Dance Theatre.

Carry on to the Noordeinde Palace, the home of Queen Beatrix, which is a grand building and a local landmark in its own right. The Queen receives ambassadors and visiting heads of state in this palace, and when the flag is fluttering on its grand dome, it means she is in residence.

A brief stop at the Historical Museum is enough to acquaint yourself with Holland's history and past, illustrated by a rather interesting collection of documents. A short walk across the Plein and it is time for a coffee or beer at one of the smart cafes in the Lange Woorhout. A short tram ride brings you to another famous town landmark, the celebrated Gemeente Museum which features a large Mondrian exhibition every December.

The Gemeente Museum, an imposing building set in the midst of carefully landscaped and flowery gardens, looks rather quiet and unpretentious. But the International Court of Justice features more legal affairs of world significance than any other institution anywhere.

The most upscale local address is Wassenaar, where palatial villas string out elegantly around the Duinrell Leisure Park – a large green belt between farms and meadows.

Much praise has been heaped on The Hague's architectural composition, with a new spirit permeating its buildings. Neoclassical vistas have been made more daring and exciting with a new surge of building activity that has harmonized the old and the new.

If you're fond of indulging in quality cuisine, you're in the right place. Local cuisine reflects the city's cosmopolitan composition, both in terms of its variety and quality. Indonesian food is highly recommended and several outlets serving this cuisine await your pleasure. While you can dine anywhere, an absolute must is a visit to The Hague a la Carte, a special culinary festival in the Plein, which features the best preparations of local caterers.

Designer boutiques and charming Oriental shops tempt you as you stroll along pedestrian precincts, while the Lange Voorhout antique market offers a traditional sort of experience, thanks to the vintage products on sale. In the old city area, shopping is still a pleasure as one wanders and browses through narrow arcades and promenades with their popular art boutiques and shoe shops.

Come night time and there are many entertainment options, with gaming, films at the super cinema which offers a choice of several different films and dancing at local discos. The nightlife may not be roaring or racy, but it is there and active enough. And it is there seven nights a week.

The city's environs beckon with myriad attractions. Several tours are available, the most popular being day tours which also include other places of interest like Delft, Aalsmeer, Madurodam and Scheveningen.

A fantasy world awaits the visitor at Madurodam, the Miniature Town which ranks high on national tourist itineraries. Reduced down to a scale of 25:1 are Holland's famous landmarks including castles, palaces, windmills, airports and train stations. The live miniature complex shows to good effect the country's heritage and traditions.

A short drive brings you to the resort suburb of Scheveningen, which boasts of the country's best beach and pier. A network of health and recreation facilities, one of Holland's best-known casinos, the opulent, beachfront Kurhaus Hotel – considered the country's finest – and carefree sunbathers who couldn't quite make it to the Bahamas, make this prime tourist territory.

Sunbathing and gambling apart, Scheveningen offers reasonably-priced late-night shopping, simple sporting pleasures like motocross and volleyball and even simpler pleasures like kite-flying and building sand-castles. A second city harbour has been transformed into a lively maritime stretch with shops, small cafes, traditional boats and a genuine sea-front atmosphere.

Definitely not bad for an "also there" city!

13

A Dance on the Elbe

A dance on the Elbe – it was sheer bliss.

The cold wind that was an agony on the face had subsided and now there was only mellow evening sunshine and the sound of disturbed water.

It was one of the world's most scenic excursions. Sailing upstream under the Blue Wonder Bridge aboard one of the world's oldest paddle-steamers, taking in the beauty of the Elbe valley, is definitely the right tonic for any weary soul. Grand city monuments looked down on expansive green steppes that tapered down to the river on both sides, as we chugged along.

They don't call it the "Florence of the Elbe" for nothing. Set against a scenic background is an inexhaustible amount of art, science and dynamic industry – reason enough for the city being ranked as the ninth largest international tourist centre. And reason enough to visit.

Their domes and steeples piercing the sky, imposing old structures greet you at every turn. And the first timer's first impression is shaped by the skilled architecture that's created a fusion between the old and the new, paying tribute to a progressive city, still in transition.

Much of Dresden's beauty stems from its historical monuments. The airiness of the Zwinger; the proud majesty of the Cathedral (the Hofkirche), the magnificent Opera House built by Gottfried Semper, the grand Bruhl Terrace with its view of the city and the green, meadow-lined Elbe River and the robust beauty of the slopes above the Blue Wonder Bridge, are all local gems and part of the canvass of this beautiful city.

The long list of beautiful places also includes Frauenkirche, which after its complex reconstruction aimed at restoring it to its former glory, is an architectural marvel. Then there is the Church. Attacked often in its long history, the Church was burnt down in 1945 and Dresden had was robbed of its most famous landmark. Now restored, it is enriching the city as it has always done.

Dresden found what the whole world was seeking – Europe's first hard porcelain – shrewdly hidden from sight below the Balcony of Europe. Thereafter, the city never looked back. How could it? It made the world's first reflex camera, was home to the world's first mineral water factory, made the world's first portable typewriters and the first coffee filters. It built the world's first suspension railway and flagged off the first German engine on Germany's first long-distance railway. It also invented the first European porcelain and today has the world's largest porcelain collection. The city is also a major producer of micro-ships. For good measure, it also invented the chocolate bar.

The romantic dinner river cruise had seen me progressively getting into the swing of things, thanks in equal measure to the copious amounts of beer going around and to my singularly good fortune in befriending a gorgeous looking Russian lady. She was a St. Petersburg-based travel agent and was visiting Dresden to attend a travel mart – without her husband, as she'd thoughtfully informed me. Encouraged by this useful and welcome bit of information, I found myself taking more interest in her than I normally do in married women. As I said, a sense of well-being was propelling me. Fulfilling my solemn duty as an international travel journalist, I got busy regaling her with all manner of travel anecdotes and adventures, enjoying the fact that she appeared visibly impressed. She must have been, because she was touching me lightly on my shoulder while she talked and her smiles were becoming as large as the state of Saxony.

Just as I was silently congratulating myself for possessing such innate charm and for my sudden upturn of fortune, we were interrupted and swept off our feet – literally – by four buxom, blonde ladies, who smiled at me, said something I didn't understand and then led us to the centre of the deck area which was doubling up as a makeshift stage. They had these three guys there, wearing ridiculous coats and even more ridiculous hats with feathers, belting out their stuff with a guitar and drums. So loud and awful was their music, it's a wonder the passengers didn't jump overboard into the Elbe. Maybe it had something to do with the fact that the current was strong and the water icy cold. Or the fact that gallons of beer was doing the rounds. Whatever it was, everyone was loyal to the ship and bravely pretending to enjoy the musical onslaught. It was a suffering mob taking an old paddle-steamer ride on a beautiful stretch of river.

The reason I'd survived thus far was because I'd been standing right in the front part of the steamer's deck and much of the sound drowned out. But there was no getting away now. We were right in the middle of it all. This little bit of music notwithstanding, the overall atmosphere was one of bonhomie and everyone was extremely friendly.

What with my enormously pleasant encounter with the Russian beauty and the couple of mass krugs (litre mugs) of beer I'd downed as if Germany was going to run out of beer, I was feeling kind of merry. While there were some fifty people dancing out there, somehow my companion and I became the centre of all the action. Since everyone had gathered around us and was cheering and clapping, I did the same. I believe I waved out to the crowds too, the way heads of state or movie stars do. The four buxom blondes had started a dance which involved all of them, one by one, facing us upfront and holding our hands. I remember telling myself I liked this dance. Good sport that I am, I did my version of "kicking the air", sang with the three guys who were still pretending to be musicians and found myself guzzling more beer from a mug beer that had miraculously appeared out of nowhere. "Must be one of the girls," I told myself smugly. "They obviously like me. Good going, gals, keep up the good stuff."

There was loud music, robust dancing and even more robust beer-swigging – all the ingredients of a happy scene in a happy movie. Everyone on the boat seemed to have been insanely gripped by the mood and was dancing, cheering and clapping. The centre of the deck area which had become a makeshift stage, had now become a makeshift dance floor. From the corner of my eyes, I saw that my beautiful Russian lady friend had managed to fend well for herself on the dance floor and seemed to be enjoying herself. If her gyrating hips were any sort of indication, she was more than enjoying herself. We ended up beside each other and shook our bodies with ridiculous movements, the way people do while pretending to dance.

Having read somewhere that it behoves a gentleman to compliment the lady he's dancing with, I went down that route and thought I'd tell her I admired her dancing. However, thanks to all the energy expended on the dance floor and perhaps all that beer so thirstily downed, I messed it up and instead of saying "I say, you have absolutely lovely moves," I blurted out "I say, you have absolutely lovely boobs." The moment I said it, I sort of froze and wanted to kick myself. After all, I had known the lady for a merely a couple of hours and this was surely the mother of all faux pas. But to my huge relief, she was not only not upset, but seemed tickled pink. "Oh, thank you, thank you. You are such a fine gentleman to say that. And you have a lovely beret. It makes you look like a czar."

My head was swimming, my heart was throbbing and I did what a member of nobility would have been expected to do at such an occasion. I put my arms around her and gave her a huge kiss.

The three gentlemen who'd tried so hard to pass off as musicians shook my hand warmly, the four buxom ladies kissed me enthusiastically on my cheeks and several of the other guests nodded and smiled happily at me and proceeded to take my photo for the rest of the evening.

Burdened as I am with my tremendous sporting spirit, I accommodated everyone, smiled and waved at all and sundry, repeatedly posed for the camera with a generous flourish and blew kisses at all the women on board that quaint paddle-steamer as it sailed down a scenic stretch of the Elbe, through some of Dresden's architectural wonders and beautiful gardens.

As the evening was finally drawing to a close, I started to feel a bit sad. The fact is that I'd had such a rollicking good time and enjoyed myself so much, that the prospect of it all ending depressed me. As did the thought of getting back to the dreary business of leading a normal life. Yes, though I keep forgetting, I'm just an ordinary guy trying to lead a normal life.

But then I have talked of my tremendous sporting spirit, haven't I? And to truly live out such a spirit, it behoves a gentleman like me to seek out more such occasions where everyone seems happy to see me dance, frolic and try to put my serpentine arms around any woman who happens to be near.

It's quite the thing to do. I owe it to society. And pledge to fulfil my obligations whenever and wherever I can. I did say I'm an ordinary guy leading a normal life, didn't I?

14

Guinness: Good Health

I remember my visits to Ireland for several reasons and almost all of them are pleasant.

One of the country's most endearing features is the variety and quality of its food and drinks. It is no wonder that Ireland is often called the "food island". Not being overly shy of consuming all manner of food and drinks, I was suitably impressed.

While everything was above par, a highlight of my Irish food and drink odyssey was a visit to Guinness Storehouse® to discover the aura and reality of this famed Irish drink.

Located at the heart of St. James's Gate Brewery in Dublin, Guinness Storehouse is Ireland's number one attraction for international visitors. The brewery has been home to the black stuff since 1759., Guinness Storehouse is the manufacturing place of the world-famous Guinness beer. The building, dating back to 1904, is built in the style of the Chicago School of Architecture and is a place for those interested in a variety of things that include Guinness, architecture and Irish culture and heritage.

Now, I like culture and heritage – and beer. And I consider it my bounden duty to research and write on these important topics. So here I was, ready to do just that – research and work.

And since it is open seven days a week from 9.30 a.m. until 5 p.m., it provides ample time and opportunity for all the research and work.

It doesn't take too long to find out why Guinness Storehouse has become Ireland's foremost attraction for international visitors, and one that always leaves a lasting impression on visitors. For good measure, they stock ample information literature, and the information desk caters to all queries.

A visit brings diverse rewards. The Guinness tour brings alive a real part of Irish history. The place a huge establishment, things seems to be happening in all parts of the building all the time and you get the feeling people milling about are rather busy and yes, rather "merry". Yes, rather merry as they go bustling about the premises.

Guinness, by the way, is that blackish looking drink that's become a rage not just in Ireland but around the world. If you don't know what I'm talking about, it means you haven't really experienced the world of brewing.

The massive seven-story building has been remodelled into the shape of a giant pint of Guinness, with the Gravity Bar forming the head of the pint on the top floor. Talk about being imaginative!

Your tour of discovery begins in the lobby itself, where you can read up on the history of the brewery and its famous beer. A new brewing experience features a virtual Master Brewer, Fergal Murray, who dutifully guides one step at a time through the brewing process. And you can also try your hand at becoming a brewer. Incidentally, this is something I thoroughly approve of – this business of plunging into actual work in the interest of research.

A hundred visitors each week actually get a chance to brew the beer by pressing a button that initiates a batch of the stout. At 10 a.m. each morning in the St. James's Gate Brewery, the Guinness team samples the brews to ensure they're of the highest quality before the beer leaves the premises. At the Guinness Storehouse, you also get a chance to act as a taster in the tasting laboratory.

With all this happening within the premises and so much work to be done by visitors, it was only appropriate that I plunged into the spirit of things, so to speak and sort of register my presence.

There are many segments that make up a tour. Winding your way through the building, you pass by giant barley storage bins that are so important in the brewing industry. You see how the grain is used in the manufacturing process, read up on the processes and on various plants intrinsic to the product and end up at the Cooperage, an exhibit dedicated to the craft of the cooper, who made the wooden barrels in which the beer was stored and transported for decades.

There's more to add to the experience. Catalogued here are those wonderful, colourful, stark advertisements of the olden days that extolled the virtues of beer. They provide a visual treat. In the advertising section on the second floor, you get to see a veritable hall of fame of Guinness award-winning advertisements over the years, which illustrate the true fame of the product.

Taking the tour, you begin to make sense of it all. It is like taking a history lesson about this unique drink. You begin to understand the logic behind the history, pride, passion and fervour that goes into each pint of Guinness and of the legendary status of the beer in a country renowned for its food and drinks. It's only after you have learnt all this that you can taste the stuff, a task made easier by the fact that each visitor receives a complimentary pint.

And the place to sample the real thing is in the famous rooftop Gravity Bar, the building's highest point and the highlight of the tour. And if you can spare a minute away from the beer, the 360-degree panoramic bar offers breathtaking views across Dublin city. Take your time. The stocks of Guinness never seem to dwindle.

And there's the proverbial in-house shop. Called the Flagship Guinness Merchandise Retail Store, it packs enough memorabilia to make you dig into your pockets and buy things you would never have imagined you would.

Nostalgia, history, heritage, indulgence, statistics of the beer's popularity – call it what you will, the fact is that the story of Guinness is inextricably linked to the people and character of Ireland.

Which makes a visit to Guinness Storehouse a visit to a truly national institution. In fact, it is a visit into the minds and hearts of the Irish.

Some 800,000 annual visitors will vouch for the enormously rich and pleasant experience that awaits you at this venerable institution.

I've visited more than once, and no, it has nothing to do with the complimentary pint.

15

Marche, Maybe

"The climate is good. Nature has been kind. And it's a safe place."

Leonardo Catucci, my venerable host escort, let go that special laugh which became the hallmark of all our meetings thereafter. It was the type of laugh that could be amusing or irritating, depending on your disposition. But one that could never be ignored, despite the strong temptation to do exactly that.

It was a five-day sojourn of delightful discovery in a region enriched with varying countryside, medieval towns, villages, palaces and religious buildings, all of important architectural and artistic value.

Marche was on a song, revealing its artistic treasures one at a time. Though I missed out on Ancona – the regional capital and an important Adriatic port, I did full justice to several other places of immense interest.

I had landed in Milan, en-route to Marche. Italy's fashion capital, Milan, seems stuck in a multi-groove. The city isn't very Italian in the true sense, at least not architecturally.

Unlike other Italian towns, few cathedrals and domes dot the skyline there.

Thanks to its fashion fame, the city gets year-round visitors from the industry and the Fiera Milano Grounds are the place where the action is. It just so happened that the Asian Fashion Week was on and I walked straight into a well-presented Sabyasachi Mukherjee show that paid tribute to India's rich textile legacy. I must admit I enjoyed the show, though I couldn't help thinking the models resembled 19th century maidens.

But Milan wasn't really on my travel itinerary and late afternoon saw me on the highway, bound for the Marche region. Five hours at 120 km per hour, driving through flatland with fields and factories with low rolling hills in the distance, two technical halts and we arrived at La Foresteria, a delight in itself.

Adjoined to a former abbey and convent — they even have their own wine cellars there — the hotel blends into the easy character that's the hallmark of the region. For the next five days it became my base.

Guide, housewife and a typically Italian woman, Mariella Staffolani was my guide in the region, helped along by Leonardo, who doubled up as an escort-cum-translator. He duly translated Mariella's words into English — with a little editing, I suspect. While Leonardo didn't have a tourism background, he did have two great assets — he spoke English and laughed a lot. I was often left puzzled as to the cause of his laughter, but that's beside the point.

Sunday morning, Piazza Della Liberta in Tolentino. It was raining and should have been deserted but for the Fire Fighter's Day celebrations and they gamely went on with a band belting out its stuff and the men in blue making appropriate speeches.

The area around the piazza is all squares and old, light brown brick buildings. Nice and easy. We did a walkabout, saw the college from the outside, backtracked and walked through Vie Del Popolo which is just what narrow streets are meant to be. A couple was getting married in the church and so we moved on to the local museum.

Lunch at Hotel 77 was a grand affair and conformed to all that is fine in Italian dining. The highlight of the menu was fried lamb that came and was quickly consumed with relish.

Half-an-hour later we ended up at Macelleria, at the little, awful-smelling shop of Giuseppe Dell'Orso, the "funny butcher" with his smooth talk and bow tie that resembled a salami. In true showman style, Giuseppe showed us the fine art of sampling wines with meat, thoughtfully helping himself to both along the way.

At night, when we returned to the hallowed confines of La Foresteria, it was business as usual there and we just about managed to stagger into the lobby, into our rooms and into bed.

The next morning presented a clear blue sky and our hosts were in a jovial mood, which set the tone for the day rather nicely. We drove past Cacamo Lake, through low forested hills and reached the 670-metre-high Camerino, a beautiful little place that presents a slice of Italian history and impressive views.

Camerino was the home of the powerful Verano family which enjoyed great influence in the region and built stately homes and monuments. We entered the fort built by the Pope Rocca Borgesia, greeted at the entrance by busts of eminent local personalities like the musician Filippo Marchetti, looking rather serious.

A short drive through the hilly woods and we pulled up in the centre of Visso, a charming little village strong on old buildings and gabled streets. Our port of call here was the Church of St. Augustino, which has now been converted into a little museum. The young lady attendant who bore a striking resemblance to the singer Madonna, explained the church's history while walking us through the premises with its wooden sculptures and wall frescoes.

It was getting to sunset time when we pulled in at Urbs Salvia. This is a famous little town renowned for its heritage and health centres. We were dining at Le Logge and it was good food served with a fair bit of style – rabbit with diced mushroom, parma ham, pepper with garlic in olive oil and crushed chicken liver. It was quite a feast.

The next morning we were back and the sunshine was a blessing as we trudged through ancient sites just outside Urbs Salvia, including the ruins of the amphitheatre that was built in the 1st century AD by the patron, Lucio Flavius Silva Nonius Bassusa, the general who attacked Masada in Israel. Apparently, forty pairs of gladiators fought here on the opening day. The site also featured gladiators' boat fights and fights with bears and wild boar. Alongside, lies the recently discovered Criptoportico (hidden place) whose excavations reveal ancient dwellings with baths, rooms and wall frescoes.

It happened to be a Tuesday that day and that meant it was the day of the weekly flea-market in Mogliano, a little town on a hill, featuring old buildings and panoramic views. Theatro Apollo is a charming little hideout with ornate side galleries, a beautiful ceiling with a large circular fresco and lots of woodwork.

Another day, another drive, this time through rolling hills, gentle valleys and brown meadows, all bathed in bright sunshine. The little town of Fermo has plenty to interest visitors, but our group typically prioritized a stop at Astoria for lunch. However, all guilty feelings were put to rest because of the extraordinary views from the hotel balconies. Below and ahead, lay the town and its environs, a maze of pale red tile roofs glinting in the sun.

Suitable amends were made for the giant risotto and Birra Moretti lunch by a visit to the church. A grand building with magnificent views, the church has played a key role in the region's history and today draws pilgrims and tourists alike.

An hour's drive along the coast brought us to Ascoli Picherno with its superb blend of medieval and renaissance architecture. In the centre of the town lies the Square, the meeting-place of locals and tourists and the venue for noteworthy events. Leading off from here, narrow streets hive off in different directions to other, smaller squares. S. Francesco, Loggia dei Mercanti, Piazza del Popolo – the town packs in an amazing number of historical sites.

Out we drove once again, this time to San Benedetto, a popular seaside resort. Things looked rather quiet that evening and we didn't do anything to disturb that quiet.

The next day was our last day in the Marche region. The start was quiet enough, with the drive to Urbino being a ninety-minute affair that took us past fields, the seaside and then green hills. Finally, Urbino loomed above us and turned out to be a busy little town teeming with tourists.

We walked straight in and up and found ourselves smack in the middle of town, from where narrow streets flanked by brick buildings went off in different directions. The Ducal Palace is a stupefying testimony of Renaissance grandeur and the undoubted highlight of the place. We spent an hour exploring this grand, self-contained complex with a labyrinth of rooms, halls, chambers, cellars, pantries, kitchens, admirable paintings, frescoes and statues that reflect the region's rich history.

Just outside the Palace, people were busy in all kinds of activities. The Duomo's steps were the right place to sit and take stock, and I did just that.

A two-hour drive past the sea and we were at Loreto. The moment you arrive, you feel it's a special place. It's a distinct feeling. Loreto is a hill-perched fortress of religion. We entered the compound and were greeted by an open-air choir-singing session for the public.

The Basilica was simply magnificent with its high ceiling, ornate roof – there's a rotunda above the altar, massive pillars and a roomy interior. In a marble enclosure is housed the statue of the Black Madonna, encased above an altar. They don't like you taking photos here and they don't like you making any sound. We paid our silent respects and left.

Our last stop, Macherata, turned out to be another historical relic. Accommodating an audience of 2,500, the Arena has a stage measuring 90 by 16 metres. We moved on to Lauro Rossi Theatre, very traditional with a large stage, ornate ceiling and cute balcony boxes.

My foray into this region had been a treat – in all ways possible. There's fine dining, a la Italian style, all over the region. Risotto and pasta may rule, but there's plenty more from the spit and oven. Macerata boasts of its own distinct cuisine tradition that includes rich dishes such as vincisgrassi. For starters, try crostone con fegatini (fried bread with chicken liver), or pizza with pork sgrisci. A good soup to try out is pancotto (tomatoes, garlic, salt, pepper and pecorino cheese). Main course dishes worth the effort are rabbit in porchetta cooked on the spit, fricassee (lamb, onion, bay leaf, dry white wine, egg yolk, lemon, flour, broth), baccala (dried, salted cod with potatoes), broad beans ngreccia (anchovies, capers, parsley, garlic and vinegar) and frecando (potatoes, celery, onion, aubergines, tomatoes, courgettes and white wine). For desert, go for biscuits with mosto (the grape residue left at the end of wine production) and peconi (typical Macerata cakes).

While there are as many wines around as Sundays in a year, Falerio dei Colli Ascolani (white), and Lacrima di Morro d'Alba (red wine with an intense, fruity bouquet) are good picks. And if you're fond of your beer, there's always Birra Moretti with the label of the man with the hat and moustache.

The days had gone by quickly and Marche had turned out to be a great experience. But just so that you don't get any wrong ideas, let me tell you it was all hard work for an honest travel journalist like myself.

I mean, imagine a situation where you had to eat absolutely wonderful food from authentic Italian kitchens every day. Such as, for instance, vincisgrassi, crostone con fegatini, or pizza with pork sgrisci. Duly washed down by copious amounts of Falerio dei Colli Ascolani and Lacrima di Morro d'Alba wines, among others.

Yes, it's a tough life, but I'm the sporting type and will readily volunteer to do it all again if I have to.

I do believe I owe it to society.

16

Glacially Exotic

On my first visit to Switzerland I had come within a whisker of doing it.

But it was not to be and for years I consoled myself saying that my time would come. Now, several years later, I was all set to undertake what is widely acknowledged as one of the world's most scenic train journeys.

"Pity I can't share it with someone special," I told myself. But then, being alone was the story of my life and being alone in some of this planet's most beautiful spots was the sadly cruel irony. I've lost count of the amazingly beautiful places which I've had the pleasure to visit, discover and enjoy. Alone.

So I was priming myself to do what I usually do at such places – take in the scenery, click some photos, and make small-talk with the waiters and bar-keepers.

Everyone around me seemed super-excited – the way tourists tend to be when they've been conned into thinking they're seeing or doing something extraordinarily special. Compared to them, I probably looked like I was attending a funeral service. I couldn't help it. I just happened to be in a sombre mood that particular day. But to be fair, the general excitement of the tourists was totally justified.

Winding its way right through the Swiss Alps, between Zermatt and St. Moritz, the Glacier Express takes one of the most scenic, wild and fascinating routes of Europe's railways. In seven-and-a-half hours, the cogwheel-driven mountain railway with its glistening red coaches that glide on metre-gauge tracks, traverses 7 valleys, 91 tunnels and a staggering 291 bridges. Not surprisingly it is known as the slowest express train in the world.

My journey sector was from Brig to Chur. Within minutes of starting, we had passed from an urban setting into the fabled Swiss countryside, a world of green meadows and forests, with waterfalls in the distance resembling silver threads and patches of mist resembling cotton balls clinging to the hill-sides. The stuff of dreams and certainly the stuff of countless movies.

Some fifteen minutes after we'd started off, I sort of felt someone watching me. You know how you get these instinctive feelings sometimes. I looked around and saw it was an elegantly dressed lady seated across the aisle. We exchanged smiles, the way strangers do on journeys or safaris and shared journeys. "It's exciting, isn't it? I've heard so much about this journey. By the way, I'm Patricia." She held out her hand and I clasped it as if my life depended on it, introduced myself and gave her the benefit of my most expansive smile. A minute later, she'd come across to where I was seated and sat herself beside me. Trying to look calm while feeling exactly the opposite, I engaged her in conversation, mindful of the fact that my face was probably changing colour and transforming from light brown to dark brown and then to red. Things were moving rather fast and definitely in the right direction. She'd provided the opening. All I was doing was following her. We chatted about nothing in particular, watched the beautiful scenery and felt totally comfortable in each other's company, something like the way old friends feel.

Not that it had pride of place in my thoughts right then, but I did try to do some justice to our present environment. The train itself has been customized to suit the needs of tourists. The coaches are swanky and have red upholstery with comfortable seats flanking tables and unlike normal trains, have unending glass windows curving into the roof. In fact, the entire coach sides and half the roof are glass, which allows uninterrupted viewing and enjoying the scenery throughout the journey. After all, it is the views that bring customers over in the first place.

One after the other, scenic wonders flashed by as the train traversed the country. The first notable point we passed was a little village named Morel from where a cable car whisks you up for views of Europe's longest glacier. We stopped at several villages, like Fiesch, from where a cable car takes you up for views of Jungfraujoch and Matterhorn. And Niederwald, famed for its scenic meadows.

On corner after corner, hill after hill, it was idyllic pine and snow scenery that flashed by. In every direction waterfalls cascaded down sheer mountainsides like silver strips. Cows grazed on the lower pastures, the sharp ringing of their bells carrying for miles in the crisp mountain air. One moment, giant massifs appeared on the horizon a few miles away, the next minute you felt you could literally touch them and scrape the snow off them. Occasional green patches came into view, tapering off into large meadows. And there were all those tunnels. Some were over a kilometre long, others no longer than the width of a road. Almost throughout our serpentine journey, crystal-clear mountain streams kept us company.

We chugged over the 2,033-metre-high Oberalp Pass, the highest point of the journey, then snaked our way down through the Furka Basis Tunnel at Oberwald, onto the popular holiday resort of Sedrun and then to the Valaisan Glacier basins, passing through narrow gorges and curves. Then came the obliging announcement that we were close to the source of the Rhine, which caught our attention. Then we were in the Graubunden Region where the locals live as traditionally as possible and speak Romansch.

The half-way point threw up a surprise. Tucked behind a corner, was a statue of Jesus on the cross, with a large bell behind, watching over proceedings, you might say. To our right, three hundred metres below, golfers moved like ants on an 18-hole course on the flanks of a hill and tapered off into wide meadows. Talk about greens within green.

At one point, Patricia asked me if I was a Sikh and if I'd mind telling her a little bit about Sikhism. She said she knew that there was a community called Sikhs but knew nothing much beyond that, and was interested in knowing more about them after seeing *The English Patient*, a film that featured a handsome Sikh soldier in the British army. Having seen and enjoyed the film myself, I got her drift and quickly got into the act.

I gave her a quick capsule on Sikhism, or at least what I knew of it, and for good measure, also mentioned how much it meant to me to be a Sikh.

"Wow," she said with a smile when I told her about our long hair and five religious symbols. I felt I'd only given a simple, direct treatise but it elicited half a dozen wows. "How fascinating! Look, you aren't kidding, are you?

I mean, you might be thinking, here's a foreign woman I've met on a train, so what the heck. Anything goes."

For the first time since we'd met, she was frowning rather than smiling. "Honestly," I told her. "I'm not fooling you around, lady." She relaxed and smiled again and all was well again. I remember feeling a bit concerned about how she felt. Somehow, it was important to me that she felt relaxed and good in my company, especially since we'd talked about Sikhism. Suddenly, it wasn't just a question of chatting up a pretty lady any more. There was something more to the whole thing. It had become a liaison of substance!

Rather gallantly, I mentioned that her questions notwithstanding, the fact was that I'd hogged the conversation while she hadn't said anything and asked her to tell me a bit about herself and her life. "I'm very interested, you know," I said softly, hoping I sounded in earnest.

Immediately appreciating this, Patricia opened up, looked very relaxed and started talking about herself and her life. She told me about her professional and personal life, her likes and dislikes, her great interest in the outdoors, her quest for some form of spiritualism, and about her seven-year-old daughter Lulu, the most precious thing in her life.

Our involved conversation was interrupted in a most unusual way. Suddenly, we found ourselves enveloped with mist. It came thick and fast and was particularly thick on the mountain-tops. At times we burst through above the mist, then plunged headlong into an abyss where you couldn't see your own hand in front of you. However, visibility was good at eye level. So was the general mood in our coach. And significantly, much to my satisfaction, Patricia seemed happy and content.

The fact that I had noticed it so clearly, and that it mattered to me that she seemed happy and content, started to bother me a bit. After all I had known her for a very short time. Something gnawed away at me, but I couldn't quite put my finger on it.

Lunch was announced and for once, I probably wasn't the only one looking forward to it and it was nice to be one of a crowd. Lunchtime brought with it another level of luxury on wheels, almost bordering on the epicurean. Since both Patricia and I had reserved seats, we headed for the dining car.

Promising "Fine Food on the Move", Passaggio, the dining car, functions like a plush restaurant. The menu choice includes fixed meals which have chicken cream soup or mixed salad, veal roast with rosemary, mashed potatoes, Vichy carrots, a cream caramel or cheese platter and bread and butter. On request, they substitute the veal with pork. You can also order from the menu-card which features a choice of items including assorted grill specialities like beef or pork steaks. And there's a vegetarian menu that includes cutlets, vegetables, seasonal salads, the "dessert of the day" and small cheese servings. Soft drinks, coffee, wines, beers and spirits are also available.

Waitresses hurried about with steaming food. Wood-panelled walls and ceiling which made for a walnut interior, spotless white table linen and fine cutlery, and food that belonged to the very top quality, made this a gourmet meal-on-wheels. It was delicious stuff. And on top of it, I had Patricia for company. Talk about dining in style. "Oh well, it's good to see things are 'on track'. No pun intended, by the way," I told Patricia, and got an approving smile in return. The fact that she seemed to appreciate my sense of humour was highly encouraging for a scheming predator like myself.

During the lunch, Patricia asked me if I'd care to have a photo taken with her and if I'd care to scribble something on it for Lulu. All graciousness and charm, I told her I'd be delighted to be photographed with her. The photo was duly taken by one of the waitresses and I wrote what I thought was the most suitable thing for little Lulu. "My love to you, little princess."

Now, the fact is that while I've indulged in this sort of stuff several times around the world, this was the first time in my life that I'd professed my love to a seven-year-old girl. It was an odd, yet grand feeling. But then these were odd, yet grand circumstances.

It was while we were sipping our coffee that I heard that Chur was just around the corner. Three minutes away to be precise. In Switzerland, three minutes means three minutes. They don't like to fool around with time schedules. I rushed to my compartment to fetch my bags, then hopped off onto the station platform.

Patricia was going on further and came to the platform to say goodbye. We embraced and clung to each other for some five seconds, and then she kissed me on the cheek and re-boarded the train. Standing in the doorway, she waved to me and that was when I noticed she was crying. I desperately wanted to hang on to her, but there simply wasn't anything I could do. This was it. The bright red train pulled away for the final leg of its journey. I'd seen enough sights on the way to appreciate the journey. And to top it all, I had a personal romantic – I suppose you could call it that – experience that was as unexpected as it was pleasant. One thing was for sure. My heartbeats were considerably faster than the "slowest express train in the world".

The Glacier Express provides a sublime experience, coming as close to a dream world as is possible on this planet. The murmuring of brooks in the summer, the crunching of snow under the tracks in winter, eating delicious gourmet food, sipping a fine wine out of a crazy leaning glass, meeting people from the world over – it all adds up to the kind of indulgence you would love to get used to.

And as for Patricia, well, the truth is she'd charmed me to the point where it took me a long time to get her out of my mind. I just couldn't stop thinking of her. It's all very well to see this kind of thing in a movie. You know, a man meeting a beautiful woman on an exotic train journey and becoming so close and intimate with her in a matter of a few hours, but it doesn't happen to ordinary folks like me in real life.

A few weeks after our wonderful encounter, I received a card from Patricia which mentioned that Lulu cherished the photo and that it had been framed and placed on their mantelpiece. Every time they had a visitor, Lulu pointed it out and said, "That's my Mom's special, exotic friend."

The card also had a scribble from Lulu – "My love to you, exotic turbaned prince."

17

A Tale of One City

How much history can a city take?

It all depends, really. Ask Berlin.

Every great city in the world has a story to tell and each tells it in its own way. But this particular story merits attention because of its sheer depth. Of all the world's great cities, Berlin can possibly be credited with having been buffeted the most by all manner of events and upheavals. To its credit it must be said that it carries the burden of this history with ease.

It is, in fact, a grand and gracious city, and one that over the years has established its reputation not just in Germany, but worldwide.

I vividly remember my first visit to what they call "the city that never sleeps". It was a special time because history was being made all over again in a city that really never could stay away from history.

When Walter Memper, then Mayor of West Berlin, had said "Berlin rejoice" at the opening of the Brandenburg Gate in 1989, signalling Germany's reunification, the excitement was palpable on both sides of the wall, and beyond. "Whoever does not cry now, will never cry," wrote a prominent city newspaper. And the celebrations reverberated across Germany. One Germany!

As I said, it was the most special of times. Two countries had become one once again and, as earlier, Berlin was at the centre, taking its rightful place among the world's great urban centres. For the world as it watched and listened, it was a piece of history, but for Germans, it was a heady combination of history, heritage, reunions and deep emotions.

Fortunate enough to visit just after the wall came down in November 1991, I had the privilege of being a part of the special occasion of this grand old metropolis with its grand old traditions. The fact is that Berlin's always been a city worthy of celebrations. A major European urban centre for centuries, it is throbbing with commercial and entertainment activities, with a pulsating nightlife, graceful in bearing its wounds as well as its wonders. But the collapse of the wall made it so much more emotional. Right then, during that epic period, there was a palpable sense of joyousness in the air. As a visiting journalist and an outsider, I sensed it immediately.

A significant and pleasant aspect of my visit was the company of Kavin Sethi, a senior, Delhi-based Lufthansa executive, who was our escort for the press trip to Germany. Kavin and I went back a long time, having met before we embarked on our respective careers. We'd met up a couple of times when we were both happy-go-lucky teenagers. We went our different ways, but years later, our paths crossed once again when we met professionally.

We got along well and developed great professional respect for each other. I found him to be a very competent and efficient executive, meticulous to the core, and considered him to be the best airline man in India at that time. He, in turn, regarded me as a superlative journalist. A gentleman to the core, Kavin was also a true professional. With his penchant for discipline and thoroughness, he was perfectly suited for a German company. Not surprisingly, the entire trip was conducted with clockwork precision.

Among Europe's youngest capitals, post-1991 Berlin is a city on the move. Even demographically, it's a young city, with almost half its inhabitants below 35 years of age. Showing a rejuvenated spirit, Berlin became young again, zestful and bubbling over with energy. Whether inside the old Hamburger Bahnof, or in the old German Ballhaus, or on the steps of the pleasure ground, or canoe-sailing on the placid waters of the Tegel lake, the city is captivating and charms the visitor with its historical monuments. You can't help being captivated by the atmosphere and ambience. Essentially a city of water and stone, Berlin has a huge number of historical sights and diverse attractions, as my long city tour taught me. If I'd ever needed a reference notebook as a travel journalist, it was here.

The fact is that there's simply so much to see and experience. The local monuments and buildings are many, each sporting its own long history. Among the top-rung attractions are edifices such as the grand historical building that houses the Charlottenburg Palace with its fabulous art treasures and memories of the Prussian Kings. And the stately, gleaming white Humboldt Palace in Tegel with its splendid two centuries-old avenue of Linden, leading to the Humboldt family's private burial ground – Klein-Glienicke Palace. They all mirror past royalty. The Gendarme Market, the site of Schinkel's grandiose theatre, now a concert hall with a French and German church complementing each other, is a very charming square with a historical backdrop and flavour.

My subsequent visits gave me the impression that the entire city was on the move. And it has moved a considerable distance, thanks to a frenetic local urge seen in several different ways, to catch up with and race ahead of the present. Emerging from the shadows are famous buildings of modern Berlin, like the sleek Radio Tower and the imposing International Congress Centre. Or the office blocks that gleam with fresh paint and polished glass. And offering spectacular city views from its dome, through over 30,000 square feet of glass, the renovated Reichstag retains all its grandeur.

Coming back to the particular visit I'm talking about, one thing was for sure. Kavin had ensured we didn't waste a single minute in our hotel rooms. Almost every available moment was accounted for in terms of journalistic research and entertainment, which provided a sort of knowledge platform and gave me a deeper understanding of all things local.

As a part of our entertainment drill, we'd been invited to attend a performance of *Westside Story* at a charming, historic theatre located in the former Eastern part of Berlin. Going by conventional norms, this should have been excitement enough by itself, but for me the main attraction was the induction into our group of one of Kavin's German colleagues, a beautiful lady with golden blonde hair and startling blue eyes.

I don't know why, but I started to feel a bit edgy. It was almost as if having this lovely lady join us had put me under some sort of pressure. I couldn't quite put my finger on it. Women with golden blonde hair and startling blue eyes have an unsettling effect on me and this was no exception. That we were in a grand city like Berlin made it all the more complex and difficult.

I admitted as much to Kavin, drawing a wry smile from the man. He shrugged his shoulders as if to say, "I give up on you." The fact is I couldn't stop staring at the lady. I didn't mean to be rude or anything like that. I was just, simply totally taken up by her.

Taking Kavin aside, I asked him if he could introduce, I meant really introduce me to his charming colleague. You know one of those special type of introductions reserved for special persons. "You're incorrigible," he said with another smile. "But seeing that you're a dear friend, I'll do it. But just for the records, you are beyond redemption." In spite of himself, he couldn't help smiling from ear to ear.

Introductions and mild pleasantries over, we were escorted to the theatre. Either by design or circumstance, and much to my delight, I found myself seated beside the pretty blonde lady. We exchanged pleasantries again, my spirits soared and my heartbeat was a steady three thousand per minute. She was smiling at me. So I smiled at her. I began to feel good about things, silently thanking my stars at this fantastic turn of events. Well, this was in the fitness of things, I told myself. It was quite apt. In fact, it was the perfect situation for a fine individual like myself – a leisurely evening at a historic, beautiful theatre-cum-opera house, seated beside a gorgeous lady. I actually felt like waving out to the entire audience.

And then there was an anti-climax of gigantic proportions. Just as the show was about to begin, a gentleman parted the curtains, came hesitatingly to the stage, and mumbled something softly, almost apologetically in German. He spoke for precisely one minute, no more, but his sermon was deadly enough. A collective groan from the audience signalled something was wrong. It turned out that the leading lady of the play had come down with a sore throat and regrettably, the show was cancelled. The collective groan from the audience had now progressed to become a cacophony of protests.

"Isn't that just terrible and so unfortunate," my best friend of some twenty minutes said to me, shaking her head. "Yes, it's really terrible and unfortunate," I replied, but my mind was already working overtime. The fact is that my thoughts weren't on the show or its last-minute cancellation, or anything like that. My attention had been riveted on *her*.

Being the host, Kavin was now concerned with the evening's agenda and after a mini conference with his colleague, suggested that we proceed for an early dinner and make the best of the evening as we could. We trooped out of the charming theatre, retrieved our jackets, hopped on to a couple of taxis for a ten-minute ride and made a grand entry into a large, dimly-lit tavern-style restaurant, renowned for its service, ambience and quality of cuisine.

We settled ourselves down, downed a couple of schnapps and turned our attention to dinner. The lady had asked us if we had any reservations or restrictions about eating anything and on our collectively telling her that we ate just about everything, she'd decided to order for all of us. Out of consideration for our palates, she took her time doing so and it was worth it.

It turned out to be quite a meal – Berlin meatballs and stuffed cabbage, something called Havel Zander that melted in the mouth like butter, pickled pork knuckles, potato salad garnished with vinegar and the unique curry wurst. These were Berlin's famous dishes and for good reason. Everything tasted divine.

I'd wanted the night to carry on forever. After all we were in the city that never sleeps. But alas, like all good things, it had to end and rather too quickly for my liking. Soon it was time to say goodbye. The pretty lady kissed me on the cheek, a compliment I returned rather enthusiastically and then she did the same to Kavin, but shook hands with the rest of our group. The others in the group may or may not have noticed this, but I did. This was "goodbye" and we went our separate ways.

I felt a certain sense of loneliness creep up on me as if I'd parted company with a lifelong companion. It was a hollow sort of feeling and looking back, I remember getting this particular kind of feeling several times again in my life.

"Thanks old chap. I owe you one," I told Kavin as we were returning to our hotel. "You certainly do – and don't you ever forget it," he said with a funny sort of smile on his face. "But there's something I have to tell you," he added. "Literally a minute before you expressed your desperate desire to meet the lady through a special introduction, she'd expressed a similar desire to meet you. She was very impressed by your turban and asked me if you were unattached. When I told her that you were too wicked and useless for any woman and that you were totally unattached and available, she wanted a sort of special introduction to *you*."

We grinned at each other and shook hands as if we'd just saved the world from a calamity. Kavin patted me on my back for my "mission possible". The fact is that an ordinary man like me doesn't encounter such complimentary words or sentiments from such gorgeous women all that often.

I counted my blessings for being born a Sikh and slept the sleep of the just and pure in the city that never sleeps.

Sadly, some six years after this event in Berlin, Kavin Sethi died of cancer. He was far too young and far too enthusiastic and energetic to fall victim to the dreaded disease that plucked him out from this world. But I'm sure his spirit is free.

In his death, India's corporate world lost an able manager, his family lost a wonderful loved-one, society in general lost a valued member and I lost a good friend.

Farewell, my friend Kavin.

18

Biking Girls and a Brilliant Talk

My first visit to USA remains etched in my mind for more reasons than one.

It had nothing to do with the fact that it was the first of my landings in this giant country, but rather because it was one of only four of my foreign trips where I stayed, not in a hotel, but with a local family. It was a novel experience for me. No fancy hotels, no gourmet restaurants, no tourism staff fussing around me, no travel itineraries to follow. Just staying in someone's home, having the hosts around and mingling with their friends and associates. It's a great way of learning about a country, its culture and its people.

My week-long stay with the Levys in their wonderfully appointed house in Westchester County, an upscale New York suburb, was comfortable, interesting and enlightening. It gave me a taste of suburban America, a glimpse of the beautiful countryside that flanks New York city and most significantly, an insight into the American-Jewish way of life.

It had been a notable journey. I'd flown into New York via Tokyo where I'd spent a couple of days discovering the beauty of that wonderful city. Tokyo is hardly the kind of city you can discover in a day or two, but I did what I could and saw and absorbed as much as I could in that short period of time.

The journey from Tokyo to New York turned out to be a bit of an adventure in itself. I flew across the Pacific Ocean, then over snowy mountain peaks, touched down briefly in Seattle, then proceeded to fly to Atlanta, from where I had to catch a domestic flight to New York. The flight to Atlanta was a little late, so by the time we landed there, the last flight had gone and so I ended up spending the night at Atlanta airport, which presented its own share of adventure, if I can call it that.

Atlanta International Airport is among the world's largest. I was probably the only passenger spending the night in the terminal and it taught me a little bit about things like space and solitude. Anyway, it was a night to be spent, and spend it I did. The next morning, I caught a flight and landed in the urban monolith they call New York.

The night before, while in Tokyo, in the lobby of Shiba Park, the hotel where I'd checked in, a crowd had gathered around the television in the lobby, listening intently to the news about a gang of New York motorcycle-borne women who were going around sexually molesting men. They'd been operating for a few days and their hangout was the area around Central Park, where they'd molested a man that morning. Now this was news. Literally everyone who'd seen the news was talking about it.

And now here I was, in this big, bad, wonderful city, enjoying the homely comforts of the Levy family. Dr. Levy was semi-retired and so was his wife, Helene, who did part-time voluntary work. I took a liking to this couple and during the course of my stay with them got close enough to exchange views and sentiments frankly. Being the good hostess that she was, and seeing that I was a first-time visitor, Helene gave me a few tips about the city, which included a few do's and don'ts. She particularly forbade me from venturing anywhere near Central Park. "Just in case . . ."

My protestations to the effect that as an experienced international travel journalist, I knew how to look after myself and stay out of trouble and had done so on several occasions in all sorts of quirky situations in all sorts of places, were dismissed with a terse, "That's fine, but this is New York, honey. Take it easy, won't you?"

As it happened, a visit to Central Park was just what I'd wanted to do and a friend had offered to take me there for "a lung-full of fresh air" and ice-cream. Apparently, people of all ages eat ice cream in New York frequently and Central Park is definitely ice-cream territory. Not wanting to betray Helene, I resisted for a couple of days, but then just gave in to the temptation of ice-cream and went.

Central Park was in full bloom at that time and it was beautiful. With some 37 million annual visitors, it is the most visited urban park in America. It is almost entirely landscaped and has ten kilometres of drives, several lakes and ponds, walking trails, bridle paths, two ice-skating rinks, the Central Park Zoo, the Central Park Conservatory Garden, a wildlife sanctuary, several auditoria, and a large area of natural woods, among other features. Not surprisingly, it is the haunt of walkers, joggers, loungers, picnickers and those just seeking an escape from the urban chaos.

It was as if all of Manhattan was there that evening. There were the proverbial joggers, walkers, power-walkers, bicyclists, skateboarders and loiterers like myself, but there was no sign of ferocious-looking young women prowling around to molest men. I tried to find them. I honestly did. Literally hustling my friend along, I walked up and down to sort of draw them out, but without luck. I saw lots of women, of course, but they were regular New York women – chic, cool, of all ages, but none prone to jumping on men. Not out there in Central Park, anyway.

There's something about Central Park, just as there's something about Manhattan. The place had begun to grow on me. Needless to say, Helene wasn't amused at my little escapade, if I may call it that. In fact she was downright upset and it took me two hours and two cups of awful-tasting herbal tea to calm her down.

I spent the next three or four days taking in the delights of New York city and was seduced by its charm the way millions of visitors have been. My dear friend, Nami, a permanent resident of the city, came to see me, and drove me around to see the sights, so to speak.

Not for nothing is New York known as the "Big Apple". Even a brief encounter leaves a lasting impression that's something between awe and admiration and you learn why this became the centre of all modern urban activity. The city has an eerie, gravitational pull. It must have, for how else can you explain the mad rush that leads not just Americans, but foreigners from all around the world to descend here with high hopes and expectations. Getting to the Big Apple is journey's end. The rich and the famous, young and old, affluent and poor, outlandish and staid, all flock here to become a part of the great circus that is the Big Apple.

And once they get here, they tend to stay, for the city's wonders exceed expectations. Every facet draws attention. The fantastic skyline, the wonderful hotels and restaurants, the theatres, museums and cultural centres, the myriad sightseeing attractions, the chic boutiques and the famous architectural maze – all are intrinsic parts of the city, little pieces of a giant canvas painting.

This is a pulsating, dynamic, heart-of-the-world city that changes its face daily, providing fresh opportunities, adventures and enjoyment at every turn, in all its boroughs.

As the locals say, you either love it or hate it, but you can't quite ignore it. And to this I want to add my own little belief. You can't experience the city on your own terms. The key to enjoying it is to accept all its quirks and charms and just soak up the experience.

Going back in history, New York's origins can be traced to the first colonists who arrived here in 1624. The territory had been claimed by Holland and in 1626 a Dutchman, Peter Miniut, occupied this promising piece of real estate and negotiated the now famous purchase of Manhattan island from the native inhabitants. That's how the whole story began.

Today it has come a long way from those times. This is a huge, proud, arrogant city that always wanted to be all things to all people and it has succeeded. Essentially it is a city of commerce and commercial values have superseded all other values, almost to the point where many find them somewhat overpowering. But then the city has never put on a show of excessive gentility. Rather, the preference has always been for the new, the large, the prosperous and the fashionable. This best sums up the city's story, especially Manhattan, its throbbing soul.

One of the first impressions to hit the visitor is the city's melting-pot character, what with Puerto Ricans, Mexicans, Italians, Chinese, Indians and Greeks, among others, rubbing shoulders with local Americans. It is this diversity that defines the city's character. While New York may not be the centre of the universe, it does occupy centre stage in the world's imagination. What happens here financially and culturally, sets the pace for other American and world cities. Despite several attempts to imitate, no other city has quite the style and sheer diversity of the Big Apple.

An impression that is glaringly obvious is the level of urban development. New York is among the world's most planned cities, its straight streets providing impressive vistas. Don't expect great aerial views like the boulevards of Paris, or Rome's monuments, but you'll admire the neat, ramrod straight views that stretch from river to river and the skyscrapers that want to defy the heavens. There is Midtown Manhattan, Downtown Manhattan, Uptown Manhattan, the Bronx, Brooklyn, Queens and Staten Island. All these areas have their share of skyscrapers, with the East Area packing a staggering number of architectural and financial landmarks.

And for some numbers. The city's attractions include some 400 art galleries, 65 bridges, 17,000 eating establishments, 150 museums, 200 skyscrapers, 51 historic districts, and 780 landmark buildings. And they're still counting. As you've perhaps gathered by now, I was quite impressed by the city and conveyed this to my local friends.

What with all my wandering around and dabbling in different pursuits, a week passed rather quickly and all too soon it was time to pack my bags, say my goodbyes and move on.

As it happened, my last night there presented a rare and somewhat special adventure. I don't know if it was with my moral self-preservation in mind, or just a sense of hospitality that prompted the Levys to invite me to join them in attending a function at their local synagogue. A famous guest speaker – I think his name was Prof. Bloom, a former Ambassador – was going to address the congregation and almost all the Jews of the neighbourhood were expected to attend.

I felt a bit awkward and told my hosts that it might not be a good idea to have me around at their synagogue, with my turban and beard and all. After all, the close-knit New York Jewish community was hardly expected to know about Sikhs and could be forgiven for mistaking me for a not-so-desirable foreigner. It's sad, but that's the way the world seems to have become. But the Levys didn't seem too bothered and I was keen to get back into Helene's good books, so I agreed to accompany them and off we went.

It was quite a large gathering. Not having met any or spent any great length of time with Jews, I was quite ignorant of their faith and customs and I considered this outing to be a handy learning opportunity. The local rabbi initiated proceedings by welcoming everyone and making some standard community announcements, went over the events slated for the next few weeks and then introduced the guest speaker.

Prof. Bloom took the stage and rendered what I can only describe as a wonderfully powerful talk that covered many matters of significance to Jews. He touched upon topics such as the relations between Israeli and American Jews, traced Israel's recent military history and the region's complex politics. The journalist in me took over and I found myself listening intently to the gentleman, impressed by his easy-flowing manner of talking and obvious knowledge of the subject. I must confess it was one of the most powerful lectures I'd had the pleasure of listening to. I found its contents very interesting and informative.

Once the talk was over, the good Professor mingled with the crowd, the congregation milled about and interacted with one another. I was sort of spotted. I could see a few people whispering in the rabbi's ears, who in turn came over and whispered in Dr. Levy's ears. Now it was Dr. Levy's turn to whisper in the rabbi's ear. Finally, both men nodded and the rabbi came up to me.

"Welcome to our synagogue, my friend. I understand you're a visitor from India. Fascinating country. By the way, how did you find the evening's proceedings?" When I told him I really enjoyed Prof. Bloom's talk, he strode off and brought the man himself, who he introduced to the Levys and me.

"That was one interesting speech, Professor. Very powerful, very informative and if I may say so, highly motivating," I said.

I'd said this without thinking, but meant it. The Professor looked to be in deep thought for a moment and seemed visibly pleased. "Thank you, thank you my friend. What did you find motivating about it?" he asked with a smile. When I told him it was the fact that he espoused the cause of Jews so passionately and touched so strongly on subjects of which Jews could be proud, he smiled again. "The fact is Professor, I feel motivated to give a talk in this manner one day for the betterment of my own community." He could see that I meant what I said and he looked visibly moved.

"You will, my friend. That day will come and if possible, I'd like to be there to hear you talk because in you I can see a small fire burning. Basically, it's up to you to decide what to do with that fire." He shook my hands warmly and bade me well. So did a few other members of the congregation.

As we were leaving, the rabbi came up to me. "I can't say this for a fact, of course, but I think you're the first Sikh to have ever entered the doors of this synagogue and given us the pleasure of his company. How does that feel?"

It felt a bit different and special. And as for the "small fire", it's still burning.

So, one day, maybe.

19

Shalom

You don't get to see too many Sikhs in Israel.

It's a small, and in my opinion, beautiful country with a religious heritage perhaps not to be found anywhere else. As is well-known, over the centuries, the land that is present-day Israel has been witness to momentous events of history. Having been a centre of three of the world's great religions – Judaism, Christianity and Islam – Jerusalem ranks among the world's most religiously significant cities, if not the most significant. And Israel itself carries large amounts of religious sentiment.

Something I've learnt to admire over the years is people who take pride in their religion and heritage. In Israel I saw Jews who were immensely proud to be Jews. In the same vein, I saw Christians and Muslims who were obviously proud of their religion. For me, this is a significant aspect of life and one to be cherished. It set the tone for my visit.

Shortly after arriving in the country, our group of Indian journalists had driven to Eilat, which must surely be one of the world's most charming sea-side resorts. It is the kind of place you want to be in if you're on a holiday and determined to enjoy in full the bounties of the sea. Located at the northern tip of the Red Sea, Eilat presents spectacular scenery. Nature's bounties can be seen in the form of violet-hued desert mountains meeting white sands, besides a coral-filled sea. It is the typical picture-postcard land, if ever there was one.

The resort is next to the Red Sea, which offers exciting experiences in, on and under the water. Warm temperatures make the water inviting for swimming and have endowed it with rich corals and other marine life. The sea has also bestowed the resort with great natural offerings in the form of powdery beaches, crystal clear waters that reveal myriad fish and other sea animals, excellent seafood and a salubrious climate.

According to historians, long time ago, Solomon and Sheba held their legendary tryst here. Today Eilat's magnificent sea-face, rugged inner mountainscape and sunny climate have made it a favourite gateway for fun-seekers – the young and the young-at-heart. I believe I fit into one of these categories, though I don't know exactly which one.

The scene that greets the visitor is of sun-kissed beaches, swaying palms, a rainbow of sails and gleaming white hotels with their balconies angled towards the jewel-like sea. If all this isn't enough, Eilat enjoys 359 annual sunny days that draw thousands of snow birds from Northern Europe, eager to escape their harsh winters and frolic in sylvan surroundings.

A day spent watching diverse marine life from a glass-bottomed boat and then in a well-stocked aquarium, followed by a long walk along the sea-face, had engendered in me a certain appetite for food that almost bordered on being starved. After all, someone had to do justice to Israel's famed dairy products and Eilat's famous seafood – It might as well be us. We ended up dining at an upscale restaurant that was actually an old boat that had been decommissioned and converted into an eatery and bar.

Thanks to my turban, we'd been instantly noticed. While we were placing our order – and making a big deal of it too – a young Indian waiter suddenly appeared out of nowhere and placed a platter of snacks before us. "With best compliments from India," he said grinning from ear-to-ear and fled before any of us could even thank him.

There was a group of workers from Punjab – you just can't stop them from appearing all over the place – who'd come to Israel and were working on assorted jobs in the restaurant. Spotting me and the other Indians on their food boat, they'd thoughtfully extended a gesture of welcome and given us the gift.

It was a nice gesture and gave a nice feeling to us. We were all touched. And as for the snack, well, the kebabs were as delicious as any we had eaten.

A couple of days later I landed in another beautiful part of Israel, and smack into an adventure I'll never forget. You might as well say it could have happened only to me! Well, happen it did, and I've survived to tell this delightful tale.

The Dead Sea region is one of the world's truly exceptional places. Here, at the lowest point on earth – 400 metres below sea level – at the world's saltiest and most mineral-rich expanse of water, you find a flourishing wellness industry, with health and beauty resorts doing roaring business. And all this is thanks to the bounties bestowed in the form of the mineral-rich Dead Sea water and health-giving springs, the famous therapeutic mud and clear sun's rays that, combined together, present a high-end wellness and rejuvenation package.

Also known as the Salt Sea, the Dead Sea got its sombre name thanks to the fact that nothing lives in it owing to its 30 per cent concentration of salts and minerals like potassium, magnesium, bromine and calcium, all of which happen to be important for cell metabolism. This makes the water ten times more saline than other seas, creating the water's phenomenal buoyancy, which keeps everything and everyone afloat.

From the Jordan River at its northern point to Sodom at the southern-most tip, the Dead Sea coast is dotted with spas and nature-care centres engaged in the business of making the body beautiful by skilfully exploiting the region's extraordinarily rich mineral wealth and benefits of the soil. The hotel spas also offer mineral-rich mud-pack treatments and underwater and normal massages. Pampering clients are a host of recreation therapy techniques that range from treatments concentrating on the application of the minerals to peloid mud-packs and wraps, bathing in mineral-rich water pools fed by sulphur springs and programmed exposure to the sun. They've got just about everything needed for rejuvenating their guests. All the big hotels also have spa pools filled with piped-in Dead Sea water.

Historical records show that the local health and therapy services have always been of the highest order. Ancient legends say that Cleopatra was among the first royals to exploit the therapeutic benefits of the Dead Sea mud. The Biblical kings, David and Solomon also patronized the local cure centres. With such a long history before me, I could hardly be a spoilsport and miss out from doing my little participatory bit.

Well, I didn't miss out. That's for sure. My personal wellness experience in the Dead Sea Region was of the sort that can bring you down to earth, and take you into a fantasy world at the same time. Things had started innocuously enough. At the hotel's spa I had floated in the buoyant water like everyone else, except that my hair was the longest among the men around. It was fine. And the feeling of just floating around without effort is something you have to actually experience to understand.

But my swimming, or should I say floating, session was nothing compared to my next adventure. I'd signed up for the mud wrap session, with a little gentle persuasion I must confess, from the pretty lady behind the spa counter. She smiled and looked me directly. "Welcome Sir, I hope you will enjoy yourself here. By the way, I strongly recommend the mud pack. It's one of this region's great services." She smiled so sweetly at me that I found myself saying, "Oh, why not – after all I'm not an international travel journalist for nothing. How can I write about such things if I haven't personally experienced them?" "That's wonderful," she replied, pleased that her efforts had borne results. "I think you'll find this an experience to remember." Her smile had got bigger and brighter. "Let's get the formalities out of the way. Please go through these documents and register yourself." I don't quite know if I imagined it, but I felt as if all the staff members were watching me, and there was this buzz that went around the establishment about my actions.

Well, the die was cast and I was "on". The proceedings started without any fuss. It's quite a ritual actually. They cover you with their famous black mud, wrap you like a mummy and then leave you all trussed up for a while. I noticed there were two girls and a man in the team and they seemed excited for some reason. And they kept smiling at one another and at me.

"Nice, friendly bunch," I told myself. One of them asked me if I'd like a moderate amount of mud onto me or did I want to get adventurous and opt for the special pack. "Oh I'll go for the special," I told her and tried to look as calm as it is possible when you're lying in a spa in a foreign country, getting yourself covered with mud. This seemed to add to their excitement. Apparently they had different packages and the one applied to me was one of the more, should we say daring ones, involving more than the usual quantity of mud.

I should have caught on that something a little out of the ordinary was going on, but didn't. And in any case I didn't want to look nervous. It was a matter of honour, you see. My reputation as a veteran travel journalist and international traveller was at stake. It was imperative that I remain totally cool. "What's a little extra mud for an enlightened, seasoned travel-journalist and traveller like myself," I declared softly to my audience. They seemed to be in total agreement, if going by their smiles was any indication.

So they continued with the treatment and I found myself enjoying the strange pleasure of being covered with the finest quality Dead Sea mud. Or should I say a lot of the finest quality Dead Sea mud.

I didn't make anything of it at the time, but did notice that one by one, almost the entire spa staff made it a point to drop in and have a look at me. And they all smiled at me as if I was a long-lost cousin just rescued from a desert island. On my part I was all grace and charm, smiled at everyone and quietly enjoyed all the fuss.

As I was leaving, the team was joined by some other colleagues for my send-off – the way they do for dignitaries. Thanking them for the special pack, I casually asked if they were always so obliging to their guests. "Oh yes, we always try to be helpful, but in some cases, we go out of our way to provide something special to special people," one of the girls revealed, while the others giggled. "Oh, but I'm not special," I said with whatever tiny bit of modesty I could muster up in those circumstances. "Oh yes, you are," another girl gushed. "You've got a pleasant eyes like we've never seen before, your hair is longer than ours and you seem to be rather proud of it. That makes you very special indeed."

I took that as a compliment from the bunch of beautiful girls, in one of the world's most unique and mystical places. Though I'd been the source of much mirth and merriment for the team, the fact that it had all been initiated by some factors that showed me in a good light, and that it had been done in good humour, and I had been singled out and labelled "very special" was enough for me to feel some warmth and glow. And that had nothing to do with any minerals.

Thanks to its unique physical composition, the Dead Sea continues to hold our interest and imagination the way it has done for centuries.

And, as I found, it can be particularly attractive for those willing to let their hair down.

20

Bushmen and Jungle Skills

"It's all a question of jungle skills. Of out-thinking and outsmarting the animals! They're a part of the intricate system of the jungle. They're there for a purpose. They're meant to be there. How much experience you've got of the wilderness and its ways determines how much jungle skill you've acquired, which in turn determines how successfully you can assert your authority out here in the wild."

We heard him patiently. Not that we had an alternative, really. Listening to him drone on, one thing had become clear. Our friendly ranger could never be accused of possessing false modesty. He probably didn't even know the meaning of the word modesty. He'd gone on and on about his life in the wilderness, about just how important it was to have hands-on experience in the bush and how crucial it was to be able to understand the ways of the wild and the laws of the jungle.

But to give him credit, spotting three of the "big five" in the bush in one day isn't common, so his bouts of boasting in the general bonhomie prevailing all around was understandable.

The famous African big five comprise the lion, leopard, elephant, Cape buffalo and black rhino. Any old Africa hand will tell you that seeing two of them in one outing is pretty good, so seeing three is quite rare and special. In the space of three exhilarating hours, we'd had sightings of a pride of lions, two elephants and had virtually crashed into a herd of Cape buffalo, probably the most dangerous animals on this planet. Certainly not those I'd like to rub the wrong way at close quarters.

The drive back to the lodge was mainly about praise of the ranger and the famed Shangaan tracker who'd been instrumental in the sightings. While our tracker friend sat still and silent, the ranger it seemed was just about warming up.

"Trust you enjoyed the drive, folks. Not everyone gets to see so much so quickly, you know." He'd obviously said this a hundred times before and had rehearsed the lines thoroughly. His chest and cheeks puffed out, he looked at all of us as if to confirm that we were impressed by him. He concluded we were and so was immensely pleased and hummed to himself for a while before starting off again. "How about if we meet in the lounge in half an hour. I'll be happy to answer any questions you may have, or tell you whatever you may want to know about the bush, its wild inhabitants and their way of life."

Resigned to our fate, we did exactly that. And soon found out that our good friend, the good ranger, talked as much indoors as he did out on the game drives in the bush. There was no escape. But as I said, we were resigned to our fate. His credentials and reputation duly established by the sightings earlier, the good man expanded on his theme.

This is our watering hole after the game drives. This is where we congregate, have a few drinks, tell a few lies.

You know. Stuff like that. This what we do in these parts. It's our life. And yes, there's been a fair bit of romancing done here too," he said with a silly look on his face.

There were some twenty of us there at that particular moment and we all tried to look suitably impressed. The fact that none of us were, is another matter.

Our ranger friend warmed up further. "See that lioness," he said pointing at the impressive trophy of a head that sat in a wooden cabinet in the lounge. "She almost took our owner, but his jungle skills and sharp shooting prevailed. That's why she ended up in the cabinet as a trophy, and not him." He paused a few seconds to let this sink in, and then continued. "As I said, it's all a question of jungle skills."

We all lapsed into silence long enough to show appropriate respect for the story, the entire scenario of this great hunt and the hunter's much-vaunted skills which had made it possible for him to bag this prized trophy. We also tried to figure out what was more puffed out, the ranger's chest or his cheeks.

The day passed quickly, and before we could say "Tarzan, Prince of Zandapixu", it was time for our evening game drive. Everyone was excited – and for good reason. There was every likelihood of our seeing many wild animals in their natural habitat.

Thirty minutes into the drive, we stopped for what is perhaps the most pleasant aspect of safaris. There's something immensely romantic about the famed sundowners in the bush. The romance bit apart, the alcohol is always welcome. They stop at a suitably remote spot in the middle of the jungle and pop the champagne corks. And believe me, it's a sweet sound to hear for thirsty tourists-cum-wildlife enthusiasts. It certainly sounded very sweet out there that evening. Our ranger friend now assumed the role of a bush barman and our little group gathered around the custom-made Land Rover, stretching our legs like weary hunters, admiring the jungle landscape and sipping blissfully.

It was sublime stuff. We were parked near a herd of impala and couldn't help noticing that they weren't in the least bit bothered by us. The champagne refreshed, the fresh air invigorated and the jungle experience rejuvenated us. It was a wonderful "nature and wilderness" package and all of us appreciated that. We stood about, making occasional polite noises, nodding as someone or the other waxed eloquent about the priceless quality of the African bush experience. All this can be quite relaxing, and I noticed that everyone, including the slightly stiff members of our group, seemed totally relaxed.

The alcohol loosened tongues and encouraged all sorts of verbal gems. "Farah Fawcet Majors found the local game rangers good looking." "A visiting National Geographic film-crew member actually filmed a leopard drinking out of Mala Mala's swimming pool, thereby confirming the establishment's world-class wilderness status and creating instant global fame." "We have a few rules here, but the fundamental rule is that you folks have a good time." "As you can see, there are a few peaceful-looking patches of the river, small pools, if you like. They all look very calm, but don't be fooled for a second. This is where crocodiles lurk, waiting for something to fall into their grasp. They just wait and wait and their patience is mostly rewarded. Something always falls into their clutches."

The verbal gems continued. "People praise Southern Africa for many things, but almost always forget the weather. It just doesn't occur to them that there's something called pleasant climate here. The fact is that we do have several patches of pleasant weather when it isn't too hot, humid or cold." "The African bush has a certain way of levelling things out. We've had hundreds of cases of people coming out on safari with us and giving everyone the impression that they're unhappy souls, but the magical beauty of the outdoors here does wonders for their temperament, and most of the time they emerge the better for their experiences. It's that sort of environment." "It's beautiful and peaceful out here, but don't forget for a moment that you're out in the wild. And out here, wild means *wild*. We're virtually surrounded by predators. But don't worry folks, our rangers are well-trained and will protect you."

The stories and anecdotes went on and on. Everything from the future of African jungles and their flora and fauna, to the latest style of sun hats and best models of Land Rovers was discussed threadbare. As often happens on such occasions, we lost track of time.

"Is it safe here, I mean *really* safe?" asked a lady who'd caught everyone's attention from the word go, thanks to her reddish-brown boots and shocking pink hat – how her hat hadn't scared away the entire game of the African Bush remains an unsolved mystery till today. "Oh sure it is ma'am. It is safe here. Don't you worry about a thing! Not for a minute. We're here to look after you," replied our friendly ranger. She wanted to say something else, but seemed to change her mind and just kept quiet.

We returned to the lodge, just in time for the *boma* dinner – a famed African tradition and one that's been featured in numerous films and books. Right from the first time I experienced them, boma-style dinners have always charmed me. It's a big deal and with good reason. You sit in a bamboo-fenced enclosure and dine under the stars. By my reckoning at least, we'd earned it. After all, standing around looking at lion trophies, downing sundowners in the bush and hearing tall tales for hours can be quite a handful for a serious and highly committed journalist like myself.

"Oh, by the way, I trust our dinner's intact," said the good lady with the pink hat. "After all, as you keep saying in your brochures, this is the African bush at its wildest. I hope the wild animals haven't stolen the steaks."

Our ranger couldn't resist it. Lowering his voice to a barely audible whisper, he added his bit. "As it happens, that's exactly what's happened, ma'am. We've had this herd of baboons that's moved into this part of the jungle and they are one tiresome bunch, stealing all the food they can lay their hands on."

Our friend was just trying his hand at a bit of humour in his customary pompous style, but the result was disastrous. He hadn't bargained for what hit him.

"Daylight robbery is what I call it – all this set-up here. You said it was really safe, didn't you?" All eyes were on her and she loved her moment of glory. After all, she wasn't the lady with the shocking pink hat for nothing.

"I stand corrected ma'am," murmured our good ranger softly, backing off sheepishly and quite red in the face. "Oh, that's fine, we all make mistakes," she replied with a flourish.

The dinner turned out to be as good as it was claimed to be and certainly worth waiting for. And the baboons we saw prowling around seemed completely disinterested in the menu on offer, or in us for that matter. It was wild berries they were after and there were plenty around at that time of the year.

Nestling at the edge of the giant Kruger National Park in South Africa's Eastern Transvaal, Mala Mala and Sabi Sabi are definitely the world's premier private game lodges, offering pristine luxury in the bush, including traditional boma-style dinners and game drives with skilful rangers.

And there's also an occasional pink hat and blue turban.

21

A Bow in Downtown Tokyo

Just a little before the curtain was coming down on the twentieth century and the millennium, I happened to visit that wonder of wonders that is Tokyo.

Tokyo is a city that defies many conventional norms, which makes it truly fascinating. Within its length and breadth, you can find anything that defines good breeding, good living, taste and decorum. And let's not forget this is Japan we're talking about, which ensures generous doses of rich cultural heritage and traditions. All this is neatly packed in the folds of this mega city.

The start to my personal relationship with the metropolis had been somewhat shaky. I must confess my first look at the city, when it was raining had shown it as a grey blob of glass, steel and concrete, leaving me wondering what all the fuss about it was. But my doubts were dispelled quickly enough and I found myself being engulfed by the charm that's been felt by most visitors to the city.

The truth is that Tokyo, gently but firmly, gets you to discard all previous opinions you may have. All the enigma and charm of Marco Polo's golden palaces is visible in the city which is Japan's political, commercial and cultural hub. And though it may stagger first-timers, thanks to the Japanese's penchant for detail, it is actually an easy city to discover. And very safe in all aspects.

Tokyo a metropolis of truly mega proportions. Within a forty-five-kilometre radius of the Imperial Palace live some thirty million people – the same as in the whole state of California. Poor and wealthy, idle and busy, dreamers and achievers – all converge here to Japan's Big Apple, the final destination for over-achievers in a country where over-achieving is a mania. The result is throbbing commercial activity and a globally unmatched lifestyle.

Once upon a time, Tokyo was a mere fishing hamlet. That was till Leyesu Tokugawa, the founder of the Tokugawa Shogunate, moved here with his retinue to establish Japan's new centre in 1590. Then called Edo, the city developed fast. Though featuring a centuries-old history, little remains from the Shoguns' era because of calamities like fires and earthquakes which exacted great toll. Twice in the twentieth century, first by the 1923 Great Tokyo Earthquake and then by a blazing fire during the 1945 air raids, Tokyo was almost completely destroyed. The city of today has been rebuilt literally from the ashes.

On offer is unbeatable diversity. Whether it's attending a tea ceremony, watching Sumo wrestling, attending a Kabuki performance, travelling the world's fastest trains, riding the world's fastest lift up seventy floors or gambling at astronomically high stakes, you can't help noticing and getting enveloped by the local charm.

The ruthless urban expansion that's seen historic sites and ancient buildings crowded out by modern structures notwithstanding, exploring a city that reflects the traditions and aspirations of an ancient race can be a highly fascinating experience. You just have to look at things with an open mind. And look for the little things – like a Sumo wrestler in a kimono and topknot at a phone booth, or a narrow path lined by bobbing paper lanterns, or a finely pruned pine tree gracefully draped over a stone wall. These are all little but distinct symbols of the Japanese way of life, of which they are fiercely and justly proud.

After my several visits, I've devised my own version of a perfect Tokyo experience.

A good way to start the day in the city is by enjoying the fruits of the Japanese love for gardening. Drop by at the Shinjuku Gyoen National Garden that spills over with chrysanthemums and cherry blossoms, then move on to Hibiya Park, a paradise for birds and butterflies and finally to the Rikygien Garden which features traditional Japanese landscapes.

Visit the Imperial Palace, the Emperor's official residence. Passing under a gateway formed by 1,700-years-old cypress trees, you enter the very heart of Japanese tradition. The palace is an interesting complex of guard towers, gateways and popular spots like East Garden, Plaza and the Nijubashi Bridge.

See the Tokyo National Museum of Modern Art, which has a superb collection of national art.

Move on to the fashionable, downtown Tokyo and enjoy the sights. Shinjuku, Harajuku and Shibuya are some of the famous designer-labels there. And Koen-Dorji street always sports a lively atmosphere.

With its remnants of old Tokyo, the Ueno area is traditional yet lively. Stroll past the station, savour the atmosphere. Then move on and climb to the viewing centre of the Tokyo Tower for an unforgettable view.

With the settling of dusk, another face of Tokyo emerges. This is the city's best hour and for a special nightlife experience pay a visit to the Ginza. Contrary to popular perception, the Ginza is a whole district and not just a street. Distinguished by day as Japan's luxury goods and high-fashion hub with the greatest concentration of art galleries at night it becomes an area of probably the world's most expensive nightlife. The Ginza is definitely an international showpiece of some stature. Famous stores edge side-streets fringed by restaurants, bars, cafes, nightclubs and speciality shops. Though class-consciousness is discreet in Japan, aristocrats and tycoons are still on the scene and the Ginza is where you're most likely to find them. For the city's rich, the Ginza is still the place to be seen in, the way it has been for decades now.

Having the luxury of time, I managed to linger and explore the district at my own pace. From my vantage point in the shadow of the Sony Building, the view of the district was about as good as it could be. Early evening bears a fashion-parade look as regally attired hostesses, many in kimonos, make their way daintily to work. Millions of office-goers pour out of buildings on to the streets and into literally hundreds of bars. And then the mama sans escort men to the waiting taxis. And all this under the famous neon lights which continuously flash their commercial messages.

Treat your palate −there are over 300,000 eateries in Tokyo, ranging from the humblest street stall to some of the world's most exclusive and expensive restaurants, with impeccable service, sober decor and if I may say so, somewhat sobering rates.

Japanese cuisine is intricate and varied and actually goes far beyond tempuras, sukiyaki and shushi. While rice (gohan) is the staple ingredient and a bowl of soup accompanies all meals, numerous vegetables ranging from carrots, cucumbers and peas to wild mountain-roots and grasses, are served fresh, boiled, pickled or deep-fried. Meats are normally chopped into bite-sized pieces, rarely overcooked and often served raw.

And for those diehard shoppers, the best bet are the Ginza and Shinjuku department stores, which offer great shopping with their endless selection of elite merchandise, including all the brand labels.

If you're a night-owl, there's enough action available to make you smile the night away. Several clubs in the city rock and provide a complete night out, including great food.

As you can see I'd been busy since I'd flown into the city on Japan Airlines and time had passed rather too quickly for my liking.

On the day before my departure, the airline's public relations manager invited me for lunch to the International Press Club, which happened to be located on one of the higher-level floors of one of the city's skyscrapers. By all accounts, it is one of Asia's busiest press clubs.

At the entrance to the elevators, we duly joined the queue behind two Japanese ladies engrossed in earnest conversation. It was my first exposure to the Japanese at such close quarters. I just happened to notice that the ladies laughed as much as they talked. They seemed to be extremely happy about something. Seeing us and realizing there was space for just two more in the elevator, they smiled and waved us ahead. Flashing them my version of a deluxe smile, I thanked them and then gave them another deluxe smile. So charmed was I with their smiles and everything else about them, if it wasn't for the fact that I was going for a formal lunch, I would have tried to join them. And I'd been in Tokyo for just three days, which I suppose tells its own tale.

"I say, that was very nice of them," I said to my good friend. "Yes, very nice of them," I repeated as if I was narrating a tale from ancient history. "Oh yes, it's nice of them of course and it's all because of you. Seeing your turban and you being a foreigner and all that, they were treating you like a guest. It was a small gesture on their part. That apart, they probably wanted to finish their talk. They'll probably still be there, talking, when we leave." The look on his face mildly suggested that he'd seen it all before.

Though an Englishman by birth, he'd lived in Japan for twenty years and was married to a Japanese lady, which made him at least a semi-authority on all things Japanese. So I guess he knew what he was talking about. As it turned out, he didn't on this one.

For my benefit, we'd seated ourselves beside a large window and I must admit to great gratitude for this gesture. The view was nothing short of spectacular. Before me lay the huge stretch of urban Tokyo, a combination of high-rise structures, elevated motorways, and a plethora of parks. Quite simply, it was a special view. I scanned the menu card, sifted through the list of Japanese dishes and ordered items I thought would project me as a person of some taste and breeding. The fact that I'd never heard of them before and didn't have a clue about what I was ordering, is beside the point.

Midway through our lunch, two ladies came up to our table. With the beautiful view and my preoccupation with my tempura, I didn't notice them standing right beside me for almost a minute or so. "Oh, so sorry," one of them said, while the other nodded. "Oh, so sorry" she said again. They were the same ladies we had met at the elevator. "Oh, so sorry," I also said, hoping it would atone for noticing their presence earlier. Both laughed, so I joined them and we all laughed. We stood up and having read somewhere that the Japanese bow while greeting and talking, I gave them what I felt was a gracious bow.

This is when my host decided he had to butt in. After a brief conversation in Japanese with the ladies, he turned to me. "You see, the Japanese are a very polite people and aren't given to just approaching strangers. The fact that these ladies have approached us means it is something important for them. Their saying 'sorry' is merely a reflection of their politeness and also of showing you respect. They want to talk to you, probably ask you something, but don't want to appear forward or rude. And they'll feel more comfortable talking through me. But first they want to know if all this is all right with you and you'd care to talk to them."

I must admit I was surprised, but my surprise was overshadowed by this certain pleasant feeling that came over me.

"Speak," I said to the ladies, as if I was a judge presiding over their trial. So they spoke. They asked me from which part of India I hailed and wanted to know my age. Now in those days I didn't mind revealing my true age to ladies, so promptly told them how old I was. Inevitably, they asked about my turban and I gave them a minor lecture on the subject. I hadn't even noticed it, but somewhere amid all this, we'd seated ourselves. The fact that I'd completely lost interest in the vaunted downtown Tokyo city view, spoke for itself – the beautiful ladies were had become a huge distraction. From their manner, I could see something was building up. They seemed to be trying to psyche themselves for what they really wanted to know. It came soon enough.

Through my seasoned, able and willing translator – who'd deftly balanced eating and talking – they asked if I was the Maharaja of one of India's prominent regions or states.

Now, I knew I had about three seconds to handle this. To lie about myself, especially pertaining to my turban, was unthinkable. Whatever my faults – variable, sizable and considerable as they are – I'm not a liar. And to admit that I was a mere commoner was something like a comedown in life and a sure-shot way of blowing away my chances of impressing them.

It was a dilemma of gigantic proportions. A dozen flighty ideas darted in and out of my mind like mini bolts of lightning. Confused, and at a loss for words, I just smiled and bowed. I didn't know what else to do.

The effect was electrifying. There was this silence that lasted for some seven seconds and then one of the ladies said something to my host in a hushed tone. And then they got up, bowed, said goodbye to us, flashed me devastating smiles and left.

I could see my host looking at me in a quizzical manner. And astoundingly, he'd even momentarily lost interest in his meal. "They were very happy and honoured to meet you. They feel you are a true 'royal' because you didn't feel the need to say anything. They'd read somewhere that, like those who have true talent, those who are genuinely royal or known celebrities don't have to proclaim the fact. They were very impressed by your politeness and modesty."

Now, I can't explain exactly how I was feeling at that moment. All sorts of thoughts were racing through my mind. To say that I was pleased is to put it rather mildly. I was pleased as punch. Here I was, in one of the world's great cities, literally accosted and complimented by two charming local ladies. Yes, I was pleased as punch – and a little more. For a moment, I was lost in a reverie and forgot my good host's existence. I was reminded of his presence when he cleared his throat. He had a puzzled look on his face. "By the way, are you actually some sort of royalty?" He was staring hard at me.

Seeing the success of my previous endeavour, I just smiled again without saying anything and patted him on the shoulder, the way sports coaches do to their pupils.

There was an awkward silence for a few seconds and then my host piped up. "Oh, by the way, I didn't ask if you wanted champagne with your lunch. How forgetful of me, really. I'm so sorry. Please forgive my manners." He looked distinctly uncomfortable. Smiling, I thanked him and declined his kind offer. The fact that I'd already downed a couple of beers may have had something to do with it. Or because I was on a high anyway, after the ladies had gone.

We finished our lunch and left. While saying goodbye, he shook my hand in something close to a reverent manner and insisted on helping me find a cab and even offered to take me back to my hotel.

It was all a bit bizarre. All three of them had been lulled into believing I was a special person with royal blood in my veins. And I hadn't uttered a word to that effect, either in agreement or denial. I laughingly told my host that I was no royal and being somewhat confused with the ladies' attention, didn't know what to say. But there was absolutely no blue blood in me. None whatsoever.

I'm not sure if he believed me. I got the feeling that he had been deeply impressed. But I was glad I'd come clean and clarified things.

It was a near-perfect end to my near-perfect stay in this fascinating city. Huge, bustling, almost awesome, Tokyo can baffle, amaze and overwhelm. Yet it's an easy city to cover. And its charm's beyond compare. Alongside bustling thoroughfares lie quiet neighbourhoods where the traditional pattern of Japanese life still ebbs and flows.

Amid all this, it is amazing what a turban and a certain type of suave personality can achieve for you in the company of highly polite and traditional people, while you're enjoying a good meal and memorable views in one of the world's great cities.

22

Frolicking by the Fjords

The only irritant was the incessant rain! And that's saying a lot, because I've always found rain soothing, charming and seductive.

Arriving in Bergen, which enjoys the title of "Fjord's capital city", I'd noticed that everything seemed washed clean. As it turned out, the rain didn't stop throughout my brief stay, which is quite typical and very much the norm here, the locals obligingly told me.

Every tourist town has a claim to fame. Thanks to nature's benediction, Bergen has several. The fact is that nature has been more than kind to Bergen. The riches bestowed have created an unbeatable package consisting of snow-clad mountains mirrored in clear lakes, waterfalls cascading from rocky knolls, emerald green fields etched against rugged granite and the awesome, dramatic majesty of the fjords, definitely Norway's greatest attraction.

Bergen is the gateway to Norway's legendary fjords, notably, Hardangerfjord, Sognefjord and Geirangerfjord. Hemmed in by seven mountains, the little coastal town literally clambers up the mountainsides, with gale-force winds that can blow a hat or turban off and spectacular views!

Bergen has been a busy little town for a long time. Located in the northern seas, it was a calling point for foreigners from far and near for a thousand years. Today the sailors and traders of old have been replaced by tourists who flock here from the world over to see the fjords, try some bread rolls and salmon and savour genuine Nordic marine flavour. And if you happen to like rain, well it's another good reason to visit.

The region's local history is as long as it's eventful. Ever since King Olav Kyrre bestowed the status of a town on this Viking harbour in 1070, cultural traditions, trading, and shipping have predominated, with the town being part of local, cultural and Norwegian history, all rolled into one. You can roam through living history in a modern setting that is just a whisper away from Norway's mightiest and most scenic fjords, justly ranked among nature's marvels.

I'd decided to brave the rain and walk around to discover things on my own and it turned out to be a delightful and informative exercise. It isn't just the rain you soak in here. There's plenty of atmosphere you can absorb as well and appreciate it.

Scandinavians in general are mostly sober in nature and don't get too excited too quickly about too many things. Norwegians are no exception to this rule. But talk seafood, or rather talk salmon and you've got their attention. Folks in this part of the world take their seafood almost as seriously as they take life itself and an hour spent browsing around stalls selling shrimps, herrings, mackerel and the redoubtable salmon told me why. The quality of the catch is about as good as anywhere in the world and Norway is a world-leader in salmon fishing, farming and trade.

That particular morning there were as many tourists as there were traders, all fighting the icy wind. And this wasn't really a tourist spot, just the fish market, but the most important place in town.

I'd caught up with my guide, Liv, and she'd given me a rundown on things local and shown me around the place. The guided tour served its purpose and Bergen's myriad charms were exposed for my benefit. Just for the record, Bergen has been identified as one of Europe's three cleanest cities.

We did the recommended thing and walked the city, taking in sights waiting to be explored. Since Liv didn't seem to even notice the rain, I followed her, as befitted a seasoned international traveller like myself.

Our starting point was the town's most charming quarter, Bryggen, the old trading wharf nestling by the inner harbour of Vagen, destroyed and lovingly rebuilt. This is the famous old face of Bergen and the key part of its cultural heritage, quite fittingly featuring in UNESCO's World Heritage List. Bryggen was the local commercial heart, where Bergensers and Hanseatic League merchants thrived and prospered. The Hansas distinct lifestyle is reflected in this town-within-a-town, which has a laid-back atmosphere and old timber buildings. Quite simply, Bryggen is special.

The fragrance of flowers spills over everything, especially the rhododendrons which appear everywhere in a burst of colours. Our leisurely, winding tour took us around meandering old streets and alleyways made for browsing, past small wooden houses which lie higgledy-piggledy, as if their owners wanted to defy conventional architectural norms and up cobble-stoned step-ways that climbed steeply. We stopped by at the aquarium with its penguin, fish and seal species and then backtracked a bit and made another brief stop at the fish market.

The town is strong on scenic views, but for me the one from the Ulriken, the city's highest mountain, was worth a thousand photographs. Those who don't want to go up can just sit on the quay and gaze at the tall sailing ship, Statsraad Lehmkuk, the local pride and joy. We did exactly that for a while and then moved on as there were other things to do. Into the funicular we got and up to the top of Mount Floien and its summer restaurant where we had another superb view.

While nature's been the biggest local benefactor, Bergen boasts more than the fjords and the sea. Rich local culture is well-reflected in the world's oldest symphony orchestra founded in 1765 and the famous Natural History Museum and Norway's first national theatre, both founded in 1850. The Greig Concert Hall pays tribute to Edvard Grieg, the famous composer who lived and worked here, brought fame to the town and whose home at Troldhaugen is now a museum and tourist spot. The great landscape artist J.C. Dahl, Henrik Ibsen and the well-known playwright Ludwig Holberg, were all famous inhabitants of the town.

All this behind us, it was time for some real sightseeing adventure – the big show itself! We'd put out to sea, bound for the fjords, those broad and narrow, deep and sheltered inlets from the sea that are geographical and natural wonders. Behind us the town gradually faded into a misty mass. Ahead and to the left was the sea, which was a bit choppier and rougher than I'd have liked. But no one was looking at the sea. Everyone's eyes and attention were riveted to our right, where the magnificently beautiful fjords rose majestically, sheer out of the water, dwarfing the tourist boats and fishing vessels that tried to ease up and literally kiss their base.

The only way to describe the sight is to say it was fabulous, a special moment in a special outing. You have to be there, with these awesome natural wonders, to appreciate their physical impact and beauty.

At the time for lunch Liv and I got separated. No, we hadn't fallen out or anything like that. Not just yet, anyway. It's just that my table was booked in the boat's fancy dining section which was exclusively for guests. So she'd seated herself at a table in one corner of the aisle, near the exit. I felt uncomfortable at this segregation-type situation but didn't want to break the system. The menu card provided both a preview and full details of the lunch selection and choices, which were as fanciful as they were varied.

Norway is fresh seafood territory, with the world's best salmon. What was on offer were sea bounties in the form of red lobster, assorted mackerel and caviar, shrimps, fried fish cakes, the ever-popular fish soup and the shilling bun, a coil of crisply baked dough smothered in cinnamon and sugar. Complementing everything was the delectable bread selection, especially the dark, icing sugar-moist, bread cake. It seems some of these gastronomy gems were slated to land on my plate. Fate was kind.

While the culinary delights excited me, I wasn't feeling good due to the fact that while I was dining in luxury, Liv had been relegated to the boat's poorer quarters, so to say, for her lunch. It just didn't feel right. On the spur of the moment, I asked the waitress if I could shift from my table and join my guide. On seeing her surprise, I divulged my reasons. She hesitated, looked around gave me a long look and flashed a huge smile. It was done and I went and seated myself alongside a very surprised Liv. The waitress laid out my lunch with much fanfare, whispered something in Liv's ear, flashed me another smile and left us to enjoy our meal.

"Thank you," Liv said softly. "Thank you," she repeated with a shy smile. I told her she was very welcome and that it was something I'd done very willingly and gladly. We both lapsed into silence and tried to do justice to the delicacies heaped before us. I don't know if the rule-book also forbade guides from partaking of food meant for guests, but neither of us cared as we shared whatever was served. Later I found out that there was no such clearly defined rule.

With the shy smile still in place, Liv leaned over towards me and asked, "May I say and ask something personal?" She seemed hesitant. "Go right ahead and say and ask to your heart's content," I said grandly. "And make it as personal as you like. I don't mind at all." After all, this wasn't an ordinary situation. I was aboard a luxury boat, sailing at the foot of the world's mightiest fjords, accompanied by a pretty local guide, having a sumptuous lunch. "Please go right ahead."

She seemed deep in thought, then smiled and started off. "I don't want to pry into your personal life and beliefs, but who exactly are you and what exactly is your religion"? She shifted uneasily. "I don't mean to offend, but would love to know. I hope you won't think me to be offensive. I apologise if you do. And please don't answer if you don't want to."

In the most soothing tone I could muster, I told her she wasn't offending me at all and I'd be glad to enlighten her on myself and my religion, Sikhism. I then proceeded to describe to her as much as I could, as simply as I could, the history and background of Sikhism and my life as an international travel journalist.

She listened intently and seriously and then smiled again. "Thanks for this. I was curious, of course, but there was also another reason for my asking you all this. You see, in all the years I've been escorting tourists and guests around Bergen and to the fjords, not once has even one of them ever offered to sit beside me for lunch. Most of them were very nice, but they never made such an offer. You are the very first one to do me this honour. I consider it an honour, by the way." We were both silent. Suddenly the sound of the boat's motor appeared louder, as did the surf breaking on the base of the cliffs that formed the beginning of the fjords.

"Are you sure you're a Sikh?" she asked with a laugh, breaking the silence.

"Oh yes, I'm sure," I said with my own version of a laugh. "Why?"

"Oh, nothing really! It's just that if I hadn't known you're a Sikh, I'd have sworn you were a Viking. And I mean that as a compliment."

"That's nice, but as it happens, I'm a Sikh." I smiled and looked her in the eye.

She smiled again. "All right, all right, we won't get into a fight over it. Let's say, for me, you're a Sikh Viking. Or a Viking Sikh, if you like. You're my very own Viking Sikh."

She looked positively radiant.

It was sublime. Out there on the choppy, surf-laden sea, within kissing distance of the world's mightiest fjords, in one of the world's most sought-after locales, I'd received a huge compliment from a gracious lady who obviously had more going on in her mind than you could imagine.

The outing was memorable. The fjords are every bit as magnificent and awe-inspiring as they're made out to be. And my chance encounter with this lovely Norwegian lady had been pleasant, to say the least.

And as for the sautéed prawns and shilling bun, well, they were as sinfully tasty as they're meant to be.

23

Santa Bhai

Though winter hadn't quite set in, the cold had begun to assert its presence ruthlessly the way it does in Lapland. Then it becomes more than a question of mere weather. Autumn is gently but firmly edged out and the cold begins to take over, slowly but surely. Its nature asserting itself.

It was cold, windy and snowy at the same time. But the little bit of physical discomfort could be ignored in the beauty of the place. It was a world unto itself, totally different, highly refreshing and serenely beautiful. I was feeling the type of elation you feel when you know you're visiting somewhere truly special and unique. And this place was truly unique. I didn't need any tourist brochures to tell me that.

Capital of the province of Finnish Lapland, spread expansively and neatly at the confluence of Lapland's mighty Ounasjoki and Kemijoki rivers, Rovaniemi isn't your normal, run-of-the-mill type of town by any stretch of the imagination. Besides being the region's hub for trade, culture, adventure sports and tourism, it's a place of immense natural beauty and wide, open spaces, offering the matchless geographical and natural delights of the Arctic Region.

Vastness is the defining physical element here, with the sense of space unparalleled on this planet. Nature is the greatest local power here. It reigns supreme and controls everyone and everything, throughout the year. During the summer the outdoors beckon and most activity revolves around exploring the region's forests and crystal-clear lakes, while winter offers a freezing but highly pleasant experience and a chance to ski cross-country across a barren, beautiful landscape that appears to go on and on and stretch till infinity.

The passage of time has engendered changes in the region's demography and lifestyle. The lumberjacks, gold miners and hunters of old who drifted here from different parts of the northern hemisphere have now been replaced by tourists from the world over, who come here in pursuit of a unique Arctic experience that includes everything from nature to culture, adventure sports, and fine shopping and dining.

And yes, the tourists do have another incentive to visit the place. They get a chance to pay a courtesy call and meet a rather special individual who lives in town.

You can't help noticing the newness of the region, and with good reason. There are absolutely no shadows of the past visible anywhere. Having been completely destroyed during the Second World War, the town was rebuilt from the foundations upwards. Physical links with the past thus severed, Rovaniemi became Finnish Lapland's ultra-modern, functional capital – a brand new city built on ancient foundations.

As mentioned, I had this great feeling of elation that energized me and so I went exploring in a rather enthusiastic fashion. There's quite a bit to see and experience here. Several contemporary urban landmarks lie in waiting. I did the tourist bit, followed the visitor circuit and took in the local attractions.

Like in most of Europe, here too there is museum-wealth, with several institutions of interest. Particularly interesting is Arktikum, the Arctic Centre – an interactive, modern, multi-display science institute engaged in observing and researching the Arctic region phenomena. Highlighting the traditions and future of humankind with interactive computer and film programmes, the museum provides an enjoyable and educative experience, and an inside view of the Arctic way of life. By any account, it is an institution of great value.

A good depiction of loggers' lives and work – a colourful forestry tradition – is seen in the indoor and outdoor exhibitions at the Lapland Forestry Museum. Also interesting and educative is the Provincial Museum of Lapland which shows the life of the local Samis and their constant struggle to adapt to their harsh natural surroundings.

With its open-yard setting rich in provincial Southern Lapland culture, the Ethnograph Museum is also interesting. It pays tribute to nature and the countryside, which are of paramount importance in this region.

There are several other local sites of interest. The Jatkankynttila Bridge with its eternal flame, spanning the Kemijoki river, the stately Town Hall and Lappia House which is a Congress centre, concert hall and library, all rolled into one, which merit a visit and stopover.

There's also Ounasvaara, the year-round recreation centre which offers the myriad delights of winter sports at its in-house sports park, jogging tracks, ski tracks and ski centre. Not being much of a sporty type, I spent most of my time in the in-house restaurant. I found it to be totally worth the effort, simply because it features superb views of the general landscape and the river gleaming in the distance and serves authentic Lapp and Finnish food.

Travelling from one site to another, all modern symbols of the city, reinforced the sense of space that I spoke about.

All this behind me, it was time to do some high-powered socialising. You might say this was my professional cum courtesy call on Rovaniemi's most famous citizen.

Santa Claus, *the* Santa Claus, lives here and is the town's great celebrity attraction. In Rovaniemi, you can meet him and his reindeer every day of the week, throughout the year, visit him in his home and office (Santa's Cave), and have a photo taken with him. To my delight, I found that you could also have a relaxed chat with him. You can also send letters and gift parcels from his main post office and shop in his Workshop Village, a cheerful complex of shops, restaurants and offices, always teeming with tourists.

I had what turned out to be the first of my two famous encounters with Santa in Rovaniemi. As it happened, later I had a third meeting with him when we bumped into each other at a Finnish function in Delhi.

There was a dramatic tinge to things. Our first meeting was against the backdrop of softly falling snow. His bright and cheery office was tastefully appointed with period furniture and furnishings, with myriad streamers and posters enhancing the colour and the cheerfulness.

And there sat the man himself, regally perched on his chair – a standard, famous sight – watching over the proceedings, as visitors streamed in and queued up to sit by his side for the sought-after, customary photograph.

As always, I was singled out from my group. Before I realized, I found myself standing next to Santa. Handshakes, nods and pleasantries exchanged, we got into an animated conversation. Though I knew that I'd be writing extensively on him on an on-going basis, I hadn't planned on interviewing him. Which was just as well, for exactly the reverse happened.

Shaking my hand, he bade me sit down and started talking. Out came one question after another. Where was I from? What did I do for a living? Did I enjoy my work? How often did I travel overseas? Which places in the world had impressed me the most? What bought me to Rovaniemi? Was this my first visit to Finland? What had I seen and experienced in the country?

We chatted on for a bit. Seeing that I was holding up the queue, I shifted on my feet uncomfortably. But he seemed in no hurry to let me go and, well, I wasn't going to end this meeting in a hurry. No way! It isn't every day in your life that you get to meet Santa Claus himself in his own office, in his own town. This was a rather special mission in a rather special place with a rather special individual. And to top it all, he seemed to be enjoying meeting and conversing with me. No sir, there was no question of hurrying here.

I was all poise. Nonchalantly, I introduced myself and proceeded to give details of myself – who I was, what I did to earn a living, why I was there and tried to come across as a cool person. The type of person who can be all things to all people, in all places. We chatted as if we were long-lost friends who'd just bumped into each other after years. Outside, the snow was falling silently, shrouding everything ever so gently.

He droned on. Seeing the long queue behind me getting longer, I wanted to move away. He must have seen my discomfiture at holding up the queue, or maybe he suddenly realized I wasn't his only visitor, so he smiled and sort of waved me on. "Come again," he said grandly and shook my hand again.

It had been an interesting encounter and it left me with a rare sense of elation. "It's my impressive bearing and personality, of course," I told myself smugly, casting a rather disdainful look at the rest of our group. I dare say, they weren't exactly thrilled at my having hogged so much attention and there was this rather frosty silence for the rest of the day. Well, I hadn't done anything wrong and in any case I wasn't here to participate in a popularity contest, so I let the frosty silence remain frosty.

Exactly a year later I was back in Rovaniemi, and of course, stopped by to see my special friend. He had moved office and shifted from his earlier location to a new one called Santa's Cave. As I crossed the threshold into what was by now familiar territory, it felt a bit like returning home.

If anything, the place was even more colourful and cheerful than the last one and sported the same happy atmosphere. There he sat regally in his office exactly like the last time. He hadn't changed a bit – I suppose a year isn't enough to change someone like him. As I approached him for the customary greeting and photo, out came his hand.

"Hello, hello, hello. You've been here before." He said. I was a little surprised.

"Yes, exactly a year ago," I replied.

"Good to see you again," he declared grandly.

"Same here, Santa," I said, noting from the corner of my eye that once again I was holding up the queue, exactly the way I'd held it up a year ago.

"It's my personality, of course," I told myself smugly, exactly the way I'd done a year ago, while desperately trying to avoid eye-contact with those queued up behind me. "Famous people just happen to pick me out and just tend to not forget me," I was thinking. The truth was that I was quite pleased with everything. This time our conversation was somewhat shorter, but pleasant enough. He inquired about my health, I asked about his. We bade each other good health and goodbye and I moved on.

Once again our meeting had taken place against the backdrop of softly falling snow that had shrouded everything, and once again it left me with a rare sense of elation.

Looking back at my two visits to Rovaniemi and looking at the two photos with Santa is joyful for me even today. It brings back a flood of exciting and pleasant memories. I vividly remember the atmosphere of the place, the excitement among the children and the look on the faces of many of the other visitors who were there with us on those two occasions. They were clearly a bit puzzled about my identity and impressed by the fact that I'd been singled out for special attention by the master of the house.

It later occurred to me that the fact that I was wearing a bright red turban on both the occasions might just have had something to do with it, too.

24

Spa Sparring

In sauna veritas.

(In the sauna, the truth is revealed.)

Well, this is the motto of the Swedish Sauna Academy, and I believe they've got it dead right. The truth is that a sauna, while guaranteed to raise your body temperature and warm your heart, is revealing and does reveal the truth in more senses than one.

Look at it this way. In a sauna, it is mandatory to shed your clothing and let your hair down. While this sounds all fine and might even titillate your senses, the shedding takes some doing. It's one thing to talk about it, but something quite different altogether to actually do it. At least the first few times.

Now consider this. It doesn't take too much imagination to picture a scene where a man with long hair and beard walks into a sauna which is full of other people. It's a scene in the real sense and no mistake. While my initial spa consciousness and spa nervousness has now given way to a certain spa comfort, I'd be lying if I didn't admit to a bit of trepidation when I took my first steps down a long corridor, to a large, steamy room filled with men and women who flitted about like ghostly shadows in the mist. I was glad that everyone appeared that way, for it meant that I too was just a ghostly shadow to prying eyes. I remembered the song "you can run but you can't hide." There was nowhere to hide. I was there, in the flesh and had to be part of the crowd. I had to let my hair down. Literally.

Well, I did. And the rest, as they say, is history.

My professional, travel-writing relationship with spas sputtered on for a while. Not given to superfluous self-indulgences, I didn't hear any bells ringing at the prospect of visiting world-renowned spas. To start with, I'm not an expert on, or even a fan of, spray, heat and scrubbing. But as it transpired, my profession of being an international travel journalist ensured that I not just visit venerable institutions involved with this stuff, but actually get an insight into their working, learn about their ways, go through the experience and write about them. It was the call of duty, plain and simple.

The result? I landed in all types of situations, with all types of people, in all manner of spas around the world.

While I can go on and on regaling the world with my spa experiences in the far corners of the globe, I'll limit myself to a few that have a direct bearing on my physical appearance as a Sikh. Because, at the end of the day, my physical appearance was the factor that made me the centre of all the attention I received.

At Rogner Bad Blumau in Graz, I did cause quite a sensation when I walked into the sauna with my hair down. Frankly, I wasn't expecting anyone to be particularly bothered or affected by my physical appearance, at least not here, in an internationally known spa resort. After all, they get all kinds of people from all kinds of places, with all kinds of appearances.

But to be fair, I suppose I was something of a surprise for the other guests at the establishment. From the moment I exited my room, I was followed, if not physically at least visually. While the guests gaped at me, the staff too noticed me, though they didn't show any reaction. In fairness it must be said that they can't be blamed in the least. You don't see a Sikh in a European spa every day. But while there was a fair bit of gazing and furtive glancing, everyone was polite enough. To say that I felt self-conscious is to put things extremely mildly. I would have been happy to merge with the furniture or foliage, if I could.

To get to the spa I had to pass through the lobby and, it had to happen that a large group of guests was just checking-in. Sipping their welcome drinks they contributed to the general gaping. I'd caused a human traffic jam. The truth is that my state of self-consciousness was punctuated by a certain feeling of satisfaction at all the attention coming my way.

Rogner Bad Blumau is a class act. Adapted to the theory that nature has no corners and symmetry need not stifle, things have been left to hang loose with uneven designs and physical proportions, unusual and unique decorations and myriad colours that dazzle and relax at the same time. It's a top-end, architecturally unique, work-of-art establishment, the world's only such habitable hotel that can accommodate five hundred guests while providing a sense of space and privacy to everyone.

Ensconced in an eye-catching, strangely-shaped building which is an architect's delight, it is a spacious hotel. The features include a 2,500 sq. metres thermal spa and sauna landscape with different saunas, curative waters, fresh water and thermal pools, a natural biotope, a garden of elements, recreation zones with galleries and relaxation lounges, lush green roof-tops of the hot springs, an 800-metre sunbathing island for the perfect tan, the beauty centre Wunderschon that provides aromatic relaxation in whirlpools seating two persons as well as new double cabins to enable side-by-side treatments and the two restaurants Iss Dich Fit and Klein und Fein.

The establishment's got myriad details and sections and features a Bach Flower Lecture Pat, an Island of Love Flowers, a Celtic Tree Sequence, a Trail of the Wild Scamp and a Geomantic Path. The swimming pools are a highlight of the place. Fed by the Melchoir spring, the spa pool has a temperature of 35 degrees Centigrade with a deep whirl and massage island. Activating the senses is the Aphrodite bath with light effects and air whirls. And forming a natural environment for swimmers is the volcano lake with its reed belt, sea roses, blossoming irises and water mint forms.

I reached the sauna feeling like a person who'd traversed an obstacle course and walked through a minefield. And then I realized that this was nothing compared to the main show. Austrian saunas are bi-sexual, all-nude areas. And the sauna here conforms to this rule in letter and spirit. This specially designed facility has its temperature so controlled that it allows you to stay in for an hour.

Seated in what turned out to be the centre of the room, I pretended to possess a coolness I didn't really feel, acutely conscious of everyone around me. I don't know if it was just my imagination running wild, but I could have sworn that everyone was intent on staring just at me. The fact is that, while pretending not to do so, almost everyone was watching everyone. There were just a few exceptions. The fact that people were watching one another in no way suggests that they were weird or anything. It's just that people tend to watch one another's bodies in saunas. Some were cool about it, some a bit self-conscious. And as for me, well, things were all right. The fact is that no one was glancing at my body. Just my face and hair. Talk about face-savers!

Next in line was the Turkish bath. Also a nude area, it had this helpful mist that shrouded things, making you look like a ghostly shadow. Once again I thanked my stars for this, deeply comforted by the thought that I too was a mere ghostly shadow. Twenty minutes later I found myself in the aroma room which had just one green light – a supposedly relaxing symbol.

While the whole environment was pleasant and soothing, I don't mind admitting it was a test of my nerves. But I survived the ordeal and dare say, was the wiser for the experience. I did enjoy the whole thing from beginning to end, my jangled nerves notwithstanding.

Carrying on with my spa journey, I found myself visiting a famous spa in Istanbul, a city renowned for its Turkish baths.

The fact is that you can't do justice to the world of spas without mentioning Turkish Baths. These venerable institutions in Turkey are an intrinsic part of the local culture and lifestyle. Some, like Istanbul's Cagalogtu Hammam, have attained folklore status. The business of spray, heat, and scrubbing – a favourite fad and pastime of a former great empire – is big business today.

Old Turkey hands will find themselves feeling quite at home in establishments like Cagalogtu Hammam. I wasn't an old Turkey hand and still felt at home here sort of speaks for itself. I've often wondered about this facet of mine where I've immediately adapted to and immensely enjoyed all manner of foreign places and situations. My personal involvement and enjoyment apart, it has helped me enormously in my career as an international travel journalist. Anyway, that's a story for another time.

The story here is of Cagalogtu Hammam. Tucked away in the inner streets of Istanbul, this 300-year-old traditional Turkish Bath has quite a history many tales to recount for those who are interested. Built by a Sultan, it has tenaciously clung on to its proud lineage and heritage. The last hammam to be built during the Ottoman Empire, Cagalogtu Hammam quickly established itself as a favourite among the 300 hammams then functioning in Istanbul. It became the city's favoured haunt, frequented by the local rich and the famous and visitors of note. It was the place to be seen hanging around in.

It still is, as I saw for myself when I stopped by. It was definitely the place for me.

Successive generations have seen Istanbul's opulent, 18th century Turkish Baths become the stuff of legends, hosting everyone from world celebrities to commoners. And Cagalogtu Hammam has been at the forefront of this elite list, attracting a galaxy of luminaries to walk through its illustrious doors. Over the years, this bathing temple has welcomed the likes of King Edward VIII, Kaiser Wilhelm, Franz Liszt, Florence Nightingale, Omar Sharif, Tony Curtis, Brian May, Richard Harrison, Volinski, Rudolf Nureye, David Brown, and Cameron Diaz, to name a few.

And now I happened to stop by. Not bad going, if you ask me. Apparently, nothing has changed over the years. The same services and the same atmosphere that was prevalent decades ago, await you today. The establishment functions today as it did in the past. In fact, one of Cagalogtu Hammam's main assets is the fact that it retains its original character in full, down to the last detail. From a tourist's point of view, at least, that's an enormous added bonus.

The entrance is plain and understated. You enter through a small foyer and a decorative main gate sporting two marble columns with classic stalactites on both sides. The door's architecture is contrary to eclectic Turkish style. On the tablet above the door is a long inscription of 7 lines and 28 verses. The flanking walls support posters. That's about all the decoration, really.

The hour I spent there was a delight of a rare sort. I inhaled the fragrant air, in fact filled my lungs with it, got myself scrubbed, had my body doused with all sorts of weird-smelling oils and ointments, burnt the soles of my feet walking over scalding hot flooring and emerged feeling like a new person.

Depending on what you want, they really make an effort to deliver. And the key thing is that all the available services apart, you can just sit and sweat here for as long as you like. A lot of people do just that and pay a lot of money to do so.

It was while we were leaving that my local guide, Fethi, came out with one of his famous statements. "I hope you enjoyed this experience and it lived up to your expectations. All your expectations." He gave me a funny sort of a look, something between a leer and a smile. I told him I had indeed enjoyed the experience, and it was something I intended to write about and promote. "Oh that's good. In fact, that's wonderful. I'm so glad you show the right spirit always. That's good for us guides too." He seemed quite happy at this entire state of affairs.

He carried on, "I don't know exactly what you were expecting from this place, but the fact is that this is one of the most famous of such establishments in the world. It has many legends associated with it and many interesting stories and episodes. I could tell you some of course, but maybe we don't have the time now. Or maybe, you won't be interested to hear them, so I won't bore you." He sounded very pleased with himself.

"But don't fret, my friend. At least you can tell everyone back home that you visited a hammam that's hosted the best of the best in terms of celebrities and world leaders. And unlike the others, you enjoyed the experience all alone." His grin and leer had both become bigger, and considerably more annoying. Seeing how taken up he was with his little joke of the day and how much he seemed to be enjoying it all, I didn't have the heart to interject and spoil his fun.

His cheeks and chest equally puffed out, the good man was in excellent humour throughout the day, and probably for days after I'd left Istanbul.

And as for Istanbul, well, what can I really say? Very few people can visit the city and not be charmed by its vast array of attractions and offerings.

Reclining on the western shore of the Bosphorus, with one arm reaching out to Asia and the other to Europe, it is a city that has embraced the world's most ancient civilizations. And one that offers a wealth of history and heritage, and holds oodles of charm for visitors today.

The former capital of three successive empires – Roman, Byzantine and Ottoman – Istanbul is crammed with history, yet doesn't seem to carry it as a burden. Considering its vintage, the city appears refreshingly young. Sure, it is crammed with legacies, stories and legends of its past and preserves them well, but it also has this certain freshness that seems inclined more towards the present and future. It wants to and seems to look ahead.

In my view, this is good news for visitors, because it adds another dimension to the city and makes the whole city-experience more interesting and rewarding.

I'd arrived in Istanbul with an open mind. That helped set the tone for a positive experience. It made it much easier for me to absorb the layers of history and heritage that come through in the museums, churches, grand mosques, palaces and bazaars of this throbbing metropolis of twelve million inhabitants.

Historical and cultural richness is all-pervading. Depending on your interest, there's plenty to see tucked away in the city's folds. And the greatest asset is its subtle east-west blend that gives everything a romantic tinge. At the risk of sounding boring, I advise caution while going out sightseeing. Not from a law-and-order angle – the city's safe enough – but because of the sheer burden of history entombed in magnificent monuments across the city. It is that kind of place and you need that kind of planned itinerary to do justice.

I believe I did do justice.

25

No. 7

I'm not much of a numbers person, but this one was special. As always, I was travelling. It was time for another wonderful affair in the few golden days I had.

Australia's assets in terms of its physical beauty are now widely recognized and the country as a whole is credited with possessing great natural attractions. The vastness of the terrain ensures that. But the beauty of some regions can only be described as exceptional and they stand alone in terms of their sheer splendour.

An autumn affair with the Blue Mountains is something to be cherished long. It's all about nature producing an unforgettable and enchanting blaze of red gold and russet foliage through the region's thirty-five towns and villages. At an average altitude of 1,000 metres, the air here is fresh and clean and the nights crisp, making it easy to sleep. But, thanks to one thing or the other, sleep was the last thing on my mind while I camped in this exceptionally pretty region.

So named because of the haze created by the eucalyptus oil in the air above the gum forests, the Blue Mountains are an extraordinarily beautiful region that provides rare and special experiences. And as I found to my pleasant surprise, a little romance too.

Comprising eight conservation reserves covering about one million hectares, including the Blue Mountains National Park, the Greater Blue Mountains Area was included in the World Heritage List in 2000 for its outstanding natural universal values. The region offers a world of discovery, with breath-taking views, rugged tablelands, sheer cliffs, deep valleys and wetlands teeming with life, and little towns with history and unique character.

As this was my first visit, I was keen to learn, absorb, and relish the experience, as befits a dedicated travel journalist. So I opted for some useful literary induction.

Everything was put into proper perspective by The Edge, a forty-minute Imax presentation that tells the fantastic story of conservation in the region. With excellent camera and sound-work, you get to experience waterfalls, parks, caves, forests, flowers, valleys and the very rare and beautiful Wollembi Pines, the sole survivors of Australia's ancient wilderness. These magnificent pines that reach a height of forty metres, were a hidden national treasure until their accidental discovery by intrepid trekkers. Owing to their antiquity and enormous ecological value, they're protected by the government, to the extent that the general public isn't allowed anywhere near them and their exact location is classified information.

Under the watchful eyes of our escort Matthew Needham of Tour Sydney, we'd left Sydney in a low-slung sedan and some ninety minutes later, found ourselves breathing mountain air at Mount Tomah Botanic Garden, where we were welcomed by its representative, Karen Gray. Mount

Tomah features several wild Australian and other plants and vistas on an awe-inspiring scale.

"All this fresh air is good for you," Matthew told me solemnly. "It will make up for the dullness. This place is beautiful, but there isn't much city-style action here and one isn't exactly over-burdened by fun, you see," he added.

Resigned to my fate, and determined not to let a little dullness spoil my mood, I braced myself for some quiet times in this remarkable corner of the world. And indeed, the first part of my stay was quiet, interspersed with close brushes and encounters with the marvels of nature, so generously on offer. I just let myself blend in with the slow pace.

And then I saw her! Our eyes locked in a mutual gaze for some five seconds and then she smiled at me and looked away. It was a moment, that's all it was and it ended. "Oh well, back to the dullness," I sighed and reaffirmed my desire to enjoy the pristine and varied beauties of nature that, as I mentioned, were on such splendid display everywhere you cared to look.

An hour later we arrived at Scenic World, among Australia's most popular privately-owned tourist attractions. Awaiting us was Geoff Bates, who not only knew as much about the region as anyone on this planet, but whose enthusiasm shone through his wizened face. Located at Katoomba on the edge of a 200-metre cliff overlooking the Three Sisters, the region's most recognizable landmark, the establishment comprises three fantastic rides – the Scenic Railway (the world's steepest incline railway), the Scenic Skyway (a cable car ride over the spectacular Jamison Valley 200 metres above its floor) and the new Sceniscender (Australia's steepest cable car ride, a 545-metre odyssey into previously inaccessible parts of the Blue Mountains). I can vouch for the fact that all three rides have two things in common – they are extraordinarily thrilling and guaranteed to make your head spin.

Amid all this I had my second encounter if I can call it that. This time I sensed rather than saw her. It seems her group had the same itinerary as ours, so here we were both, face-to-face.

"Hi there, I'm Constance and I'm from Melbourne," she introduced herself. I introduced myself and we shook hands. "You're a long way from home, mate," she said to me with a faint smile on her lips. I remember mumbling something about how long-distance travel was my middle name. The fact is I couldn't keep my eyes off her. Her brown eyes, brown hair and sunburned complexion created feelings of somewhat devastating proportions that I found highly appealing and disturbing at the same time. We chatted for a bit and I felt she was becoming more relaxed. I can't say the same for myself, though. My heart was racing like a whisky-fed stallion, and I felt this thumping sort of feeling in my chest.

The Three Sisters looked down on us. Carved from the surrounding sandstone cliffs over millions of years by erosion, the Sisters are steeped in legend, the most popular being the aborigine one. Three beautiful sisters, Meehni, Wimlah and Gunnedoo once lived with the Gundungurra people in the Jamison Valley and were in love with three brothers from the neighbouring nation of the Daruk people. But marriage was forbidden by tribal law. The warrior brothers decided to take the sisters by force. Tribal war forced the Kuradjuri (clever man) of the Gundungurra people to turn the sisters into stone. He intended to restore them after the danger had passed, but was killed in the battle and to this day no one has been able to break the spell and restore the sisters back to their natural form. So they stand there as giant stone monoliths, marvels of nature.

"It's a poignant and beautiful story, isn't it?" Constance was standing a bare six inches away from me and her smile was as huge as the mountains that formed a giant, hazy wall in the distance. "Yes it's a poignant and beautiful story," I replied with my unmatched sense of brilliance. "It's a really poignant and beautiful story," I repeated. More brilliance.

Fortunately, Constance didn't notice this moronic brilliance and just seemed intent on taking in the scenery. And who could blame her? The views from the vantage point on which we were perched were worth dying for. They probably rank among the best in the world. She sighed, flashed me another mountain-sized smile, and sighed again. We chatted for a bit and exchanged all the pleasantries you can in a brief tourist encounter. She had to leave with her group, but we decided to catch up again as soon as we could, wherever we could, if we could.

We went our different ways. If the day was about exploring nature, the evening brought refined elegance. Lilianfels is an Orient Express Hotel of true class and breeding, with fantastic views of the dramatic escarpment of the Blue Mountains, the Three Sisters, and the hazy horizons.

We dined at Darley's, an extraordinary, award-winning restaurant, and the roasted, semi-rare Crippsland lamb rack,and garlic and confit tomato were as good as any I've ever tasted. And believe me, I've tasted some excellent lamb dishes worldwide. And the beer went down rather easily, as it always does with me.

But my mind was on Constance. If this was what they call distraction, then well, I was distracted as anything. In thirty momentous minutes, she'd grown on me the way pretty women tend to grow on me in thirty minutes and I was missing her easy-flowing conversation and large smiles.

"Missing her, are you? Don't worry mate. You'll bump into her again soon." Now Matthew did have a sense of humour and as I'd noticed, was quite perceptive. But then he was just doing duty as our guide. Just as I was about to dismiss him disdainfully, he winked and whispered in my ear. "To tell you the truth, I sort of fancy a lady myself and am missing her. She's Indian, by the way." The good man winked again. This time it was a conspiratorial sort of wink, as befits co-conspirators who pretend to know everything while knowing nothing.

The night was inky black when we returned to our hotel, probably one of the finest in the region. With some ten rooms housed in an old manor, with house-style cooking and plenty of warmth, Kubba Roonga Guest House oozes with atmosphere and my stay there was nothing short of delightful.

Also delightful was the message awaiting me. Constance had phoned for me and wanted me to return her call. I did, and we talked a little. Not given to lengthy phone conversations, our half-hour chat must be a sort of record for me. I can't remember the last time I'd rambled so much on the phone. And in fact, don't remember much of what we chatted about. All I remember is that her voice was a balm to my heart. I slept the sleep of the blessed, which is a luxury that doesn't come my way too often.

Come morning and we were back in the heart of the mountains, admiring what must surely be one of the world's best views. Standing at Echo Point, it's easy to see why everyone succumbs to the area's charms. It is a truly magical sight. Hill after hill unfolds, seeming to change colour as you look over miles and miles of forested country fading into the distance in the mist. It is a giant canvass of green beauty.

"It's dream stuff, isn't it?" I hadn't seen her come up, but there she was, standing right beside me. I could literally feel her breathe. It was amazing how we kept bumping into each other. Admittedly, there aren't too many people running around in this region, but it is a huge region. Before I could stammer out any sort of response she put her finger on my lips and flashed me one of those Goliath-sized smiles that had started to play havoc with my mental faculties.

"Shoosh. Hold your horses. It's not that I want to muzzle you, but I have something to say and want to say it without any interruption at all. Are we all set, then?"

I nodded and flashed her what I can only describe as my own version of a Goliath smile. She acknowledged it with a smile. "All right then. First things first. Seeing as we've become good friends in such a short span of time, I've decided to name you No. 7 because there have been six men in my life. My dad and two brothers, who I adore, and three former boyfriends, one of who I admire, one I respect, and one I now positively dislike."

She smiled and put her finger on my lips again, just in case I piped up and said something. "And now you've popped up out of nowhere with all kinds of weird possibilities, and I can just feel in my bones that we were meant to meet, and that too in a special place like this. I have this feeling about you. There are certain possibilities. All right, I'm done now. The floor is yours." She looked a bit relieved though a bit uncertain, like someone who'd just bitten the bullet and got a huge load off her chest.

I was in a trance. A beautiful woman with whom I'd spent a total of sixty minutes in one of the world's truly enchanting places, had actually accorded me a place in her life. Just like that. After just two brief meetings in the sunshine. "Costers, Fosters". Was this wonderful or what? Was I in heaven? I mean, it wasn't totally surprising, what with my innate charm and all, but was this for real? I don't know if it was the general quietness that pervades and enhances the appeal of the Blue Mountains region, but I could have sworn everyone within a hundred metres must have heard my thudding heartbeats.

Constance was leaving. This was goodbye time. We embraced and kept embracing, for the simple reason that I didn't let her go. She seemed to be happy and resigned at the same time and had obviously noticed how shell-shocked I was. "It's all right, No. 7. It's just as well. You'll get over me soon enough. And as for me, I can't seem to hold onto a man, anyway. I don't want to kid myself that I could hold onto a man like you." Tears welled up in her eyes and right then, for just a moment, she looked about as vulnerable as anyone ever could be. Suddenly she looked fragile and I felt the wind could have plucked her from her perch and blown her away.

She kissed me hard on the cheek and ran, yes ran to where her coach was waiting. I found myself alone at Echo Point and for the umpteenth time in my life, felt what it was like to be really and truly alone. It was an enormous and total emptiness I've known far too well for far too long and come to dread. But that's life!

Our last evening in this special "neck of the woods" needed an Indian dinner and it was provided with much largesse at Arjuna Restaurant in Katoomba, where the charming owner, Razina Kher, gave us the lowdown on Indian cuisine in Australia, over generous helpings of chicken makhni and daal.

Our brief tryst with the Blue Mountains was dreamy stuff. The type whose memories never fade. We'd been driven around by Matthew in a comfortable car. And we'd dined at the region's finest al fresco eateries. The spectacular hues of the mountains' foliage, wonderful bush-walks, historical attractions, galleries, craft and antique shops, scenic drives, cave explorations, adventure activities, Victorian and Edwardian style buildings and cafes offering the decadence of Devonshire teas with lashings of cream, had all come with a delightful twist and had combined to form a deadly package of seduction. Almost too deadly for a simple man like me to absorb.

A week after I returned home I got a card from her.

"Dear 007. I hope this finds you as well, but not as lonely as I'm feeling right now. Imagine my thoughts. I could never in my wildest dreams have imagined meeting a man with a turban in the salubrious confines of the Blue Mountains. But we did meet, and we both do exist, even though far away from each other. The rest is destiny. Think of me often and take care of yourself. Contrary to what you might think, you can be easily 'shaken and stirred' too – just like me."

26

"Kuch Kuch" Kaohsiung

As second cities go, it's a beautiful place.
The myriad facets of life on offer ensure this. As does its layout and architectural composition. To put it in tourist jargon, the city is well-endowed in all relevant departments such as interesting sites, accommodation, cuisine and shopping. Which simply means that at the end of the day, you can't help wondering why you hadn't even heard of it before. But that's the way it goes.
I was one of a group of some thirteen journalists, all hailing from different countries, and the idea was for us to see, absorb and appreciate Taiwan's sights, sounds, culture, heritage and way of life. Our large group comprised journalists from Jordan, Malaysia, Vietnam, the USA, Honduras, Panama, Columbia, Peru and the West Indies, and two delegates from the Taiwan Ministry of Foreign Affairs, our kind hosts.
I'd arrived from Taipei, courtesy the Taiwan High Speed Rail and the ninety-six-minute ride, with a stop at Taichung, was as smooth as flowers. The High-Speed Rail network is

a marvel of Taiwan's engineering prowess and the super-fast trains literally glide across the country, eating up the miles with quiet ease.

During our stay in Taipei prior to this and during the train journey, our group members had got to know one another and the general atmosphere was pleasant and congenial. Having more or less befriended all the group members and our hosts, I had jokingly mentioned to them a few times that they need not worry if anything went wrong. I was a man with connections. All I had to do was make a few phone calls.

So it was a group that included a man of substance and high connections that arrived in Kaohsiung, a city of substance.

Things fell into a convenient groove right from the start, with my hotel, The Splendor Kaohsiung, providing a perfect setting and being a perfect resting place. Taiwan's highest building until overtaken by Taipei 101, the hotel is still the highest in the country and the view from its Tuntex 85 Skytower isn't just panoramic, it is truly superlative. While three corners focus on the sprawling city, one presents a pristine view of the calm, pale blue sea and Kao Port. The Skytower's got it all – unending glass walls for viewing, telescopes, seating, signages, souvenirs and a refreshment counter. All I had to do was get into a special elevator to be whisked up for the visual treats.

A hearty lunch tucked in, I set about exploring the city. Things being spaced out means you have to drive around from point to point. My starting point was Horizon, a company that employs some seven hundred staff, has four shipyards and is ranked among the top ten yacht companies in the world. Seeing that their yachts are priced from US$ 5 to 32 million, I politely declined the kind offer of buying one. "Some other time, perhaps," I told the cheerful manager who had welcomed me to the premises, showed me around and offered me a cup of coffee that was almost as good as the one I brew and drink at home.

Eager to provide me with a complete local experience, my hosts had slotted baseball into my hectic schedule, and evening saw me seated – rather comfortably, I might add, what with the beer and hamburgers – in the VIP section of the stadium to see Uni-Lions try to get the better of EDA-Rhinos. By now I'd noticed that baseball isn't just popular in Taiwan, it is a very big deal. I must confess that this sport holds no great charm for me and I couldn't understand what the fuss was all about. But I relished the overall experience.

The next day started extremely pleasantly because not only did the restaurant of the hotel serve a gigantic breakfast, but being a clear morning, the harbour view was breath-taking. With all this munificence, I tucked into my breakfast with vigour and energy and was in a rather good mood when they took me to the Pier 2 Art Centre, located next to the old Yancheng Commercial Harbour.

The Pier 2 Art Centre is a very interesting quarter of the city, with its own unique story. An old warehouse complex built by the Japanese to store sugarcane granulated sugar and other food items, the site got an image makeover in the year 2000 with a group of artists establishing experiential art here. With the harbour opened for locals and visitors and some twenty-five warehouses staging art shows and cultural events, the centre is one big happening place and a major local tourist draw.

Meal time is a good time in Taiwan. There's simply so much good food around, with the emphasis being on freshness. Seated at Old & New, certainly among Taiwan's frontrunners in serving delicious local cuisine, I gave a patient hearing to members of our group who waxed eloquent about their great knowledge and appreciation of Oriental art. If there's one thing forty years of international travel has taught me, it is that people who profess to be experts at anything are in fact the exact opposite. They actually know little.

So when the conversation just went on and on, I decided it was time to inform our motley group that I wasn't exactly a greenhorn myself when it came to art appreciation. Everyone listened intently, but it was obvious that all attention centred round the food. Well, fair enough. The food left nothing to be desired and I dare say justice was done. I can't remember having had tastier or tangier prawns and lobsters.

It was now time to experience an event of national importance. The Kaohsiung Dragon Boat Festival and the International Dragon Boat Races are deeply embedded in Taiwanese psyche and draw huge crowds of both locals and foreigners. The stretch of the river that stages the races becomes something like a giant stadium with cheering spectators lining both banks. Without a clue about the sport, and the teams' classification, I nevertheless pretended I knew everything that was going on and joined in on the cheering as a matter of good sportsman-like behaviour.

As a city, Kaohsiung can become what you make of it. It's got a bit of everything. If you're looking for big-city hype, you can get your money's worth in the fancy shopping malls and gourmet restaurants. Shopping options abound all over the city and the gamut extends from swanky malls down to tiny shops lining narrow streets. The culinary department is well catered to, thanks to dozens of traditional and modern restaurants and cafes that serve assorted cuisine. So if you're a conventional tourist, this will sort you out and keep you in fine fettle.

But the city has also got something for those seeking a glimpse at the Orient of the old. It is this blend of the old and new and modern and traditional that imbues the city with its innate charm.

Standing on the rail platform, awaiting our train back to Taipei, my hosts smilingly asked our group if everything had gone according to our satisfaction. On our saying it most certainly had, and that we'd all had a wonderful time, they diverted their attention to me.

"Sir, we are glad you didn't have to make any special phone calls," they said with serious expressions on their faces. Everyone clapped and cheered. I didn't know exactly what they were applauding, but being a rather good sport, I assumed it was aimed at me.

Everyone clapped and cheered some more and it was one big happy group that boarded the high-speed train back to Taipei.

27

Quantum of Solace

The first sight. The first touch. The first meal. Moment one.

Words aren't necessarily the best medium of communication here, but a few good words are in order.

If you're wondering what the fuss is all about, it's just this little business of Royal Caribbean International's super-duper ocean liner, *Quantum of the Seas*, that's been making waves literally and figuratively with its unprecedented levels of technology that amps up the vacation experience. It's a technological hurly-burly. Boatloads of bandwidth keep guests connected, easy-to-use systems expand guest choices and simplify schedules and RFID technology speeds up the boarding process. You have to agree that there's merit in their slogan "For the smoothest trip, sail the Smart Ship."

Well, I did. And I am rather keen to share the offbeat and beautiful experience with those who are interested in going just a little beyond the mundane daily life.

It wasn't my doing, really, but literally thirty minutes after boarding, I found myself in the confines of Jamie Oliver's Italian restaurant and partook virtually their first meal. The establishment is al fresco, the food authentic Italian and sinful and the service, well, Italian. Entree, salad, roast pork, cheese, polenta, zucchini and pork belly stuffed with vegetables, comprised a meal of some substance. In a matter of minutes I'd got hooked on to their Italian cuisine.

Lunch done, I ventured to my stateroom with a view, if I may call it that. I thought it was just a little bit smaller than it should have been, but on the whole it was supremely comfortable. The large bay windows invite constant viewing. The ship has all manner of staterooms and suites, including some with virtual balconies featuring external views. There's the Royal Family Suite that accommodates eight passengers, the Sky Loft Suite for four passengers. And there are Junior Suites for four passengers.

I went exploring the ship and found there's plenty to explore. It is basically one big high-tech dining and entertainment complex that's made keeping everybody's desires and comforts in mind. As is my want, I decided to prowl around without a set objective.

I found myself standing outside Casino Royale Music Hall and decided to grace the establishment with my presence. An ornate interior and a classy look predominate, but the music wasn't bad either, though I must confess none of it was familiar to me. The central lounge areas resemble airport shopping complexes, with pubs, bars, eateries, cafes, boutiques and shops edging one another. Consider the fact that there are seven hundred and fifty-three culinary staff – half the ship's total staff strength – and you realize just how integral dining is to the cruise experience.

My prowl with a mission was temporarily interrupted by what they call the Muster Drill, a safety drill interlude that acquaints guests with the safety issues and nuances onboard. We had to sit around and wait a bit, but the drill itself was short and sweet, not unlike the safety drills on flights. Impatient soul that I am, I was fidgeting and literally counting the minutes for it to end, but I have to admit that it was informative and could come in very handy indeed if there is a mishap of any sort.

Kind souls that they are, Royal Caribbean had set out cocktails for a media meet to greet and "shoot the breeze". I had no idea there would be so many journalists around, but enjoyed the intermingling bit. Not surprisingly, everyone seemed to be in a good mood, aided a bit, I might add, by the drinks on offer. Midway through, I noticed we'd set sail. It was a moment of history. The first foray out to sea of the world's newest, most modern, most tech-savvy ship. What a moment, and what a feeling!

Well, the fact is that it was an occasion of sorts and to be fair to everyone and everything involved, I just had to have another celebratory drink.

At that moment my thoughts went off into a different tangent. I had a flashback of my very first cruise with Royal Caribbean, some twenty years back, courtesy of Gautam Chadha, the man who introduced Royal Caribbean to India, and revolutionized the concept of cruising in the country.

By all accounts, Gautam was an exceptionally savvy and smart businessman, who had the knack of reading business situations very well. He was a thinker and had a vision of what he wanted to achieve in his business.

In my opinion he was years ahead of his contemporaries and competitors. Through sheer dint of hard work and a spirit of enterprise, he built up a business empire of sorts. Royal Caribbean today is a name to be reckoned with in India. It's the first name that comes to mind when one thinks of cruising. Ask for a cruise to any exotic destination, and the chances are the company will arrange your sailing there.

Sadly, Gautam died a few years ago. But his memory lives on. And his business mantle has been skilfully and successfully picked up by his wife, Ratna Chadha, who is a highly motivated and efficient business woman in her own right. She has ensured that the strong brand built up by Gautam has not only sustained, but actually become stronger.

Coming back to my present cruise, the celebratory mood sort of accompanied me to dinner at the Grande. Half the size of a football field, the fine-dining restaurant features a soothing, classy decor with dim lighting, soft music and an ambience that takes you back to the 1920s. An assortment of appetizers – prawn cocktail, traditional lobster bisque and truffled wild mushroom risotto was followed by the entrees – Mediterranean bouillabaisse, sole almandine and braised lamb shank and the desserts – molten chocolate lava cake, classic Napoleon and red velvet cheesecake.

The evening wasn't quite done. Bringing the curtain down on a classical day was *Starwater*, the show. Saddled with travel fatigue, I must confess I'd considered ducking out but am immensely glad I braved it out, as the show was very interesting.

The Quantum class of ships advances the cruise experience with the introduction of revolutionary signature venues and none stands out more than Two70, so named because of its breath-taking 270-degree panoramic sea and destination views provided, thanks to vast, soaring, floor-to-ceiling glass walls that span almost three decks high at the stern of the ship and are a show-stopping and revolutionary step in ship design. This multi-level venue seamlessly fuses entertainment and technology to create a transformative journey for guests from morning to night.

As the sun sets, Two70 unveils its evening persona, consisting of spectacular, mysterious and unexpected entertainment. The evening's first stop is the beautiful, dramatic, curved bar which serves as a magnificent focal point for Two70. The performances aren't limited to the stage, but happen all around, mesmerizing the audience through a combination of live performers, aerialists, performance art and breath-taking video. Guests also experience Vistarama, floor-to-ceiling glass walls which display projections of dazzling digital scenery which encircles the room. Two70's unparalleled technology, theatrical lighting and heavy sound equipment create a completely enthralling evening. Housed in the ceiling are six robot arms controlling individual 100-inch LED TV screens which feature gorgeous video and imagery which can virtually jump from screen to screen. It's hardly surprising that most guests who enter the premises tend to linger on.

The introductory announcement was anything but modest and expectations were duly raised. Well, the expectations were certainly met and surpassed. The show was superb, the effects spectacular, the energy levels high and the venue a story in itself.

With all this done – in the interest of research, of course – I finally told myself it was time to call it a day and headed for my stateroom. No bed in the entire world could have felt softer or more comfortable than mine that night. I slept soundly.

The next morning, I was back in action. For a traditionally non-breakfast person I did rather well at Windjammer, which is tucked away on the 14th floor. Roughly the size of three tennis courts, the restaurant features superb sea views and an endless variety of international cuisine. The cuisine of world was on display in the myriad counters – American Favourites, On the Mediterranean, International Flavours, Farm Fresh, Thirst Quencher, Lite Bites and so on. I would gladly have tried them all, but as you can imagine, as a hard-working journalist I had things to do and promises to keep.

So I did what I had to and duly attended the press meet, addressed by Royal Caribbean's top brass. Obviously the ship and its latest, cutting-edge technology was the main focus, especially how it simplifies things. So they highlighted various points, such as innovations coming fast on cruise ships, technology enhancing guests' experiences, special features like the immensely popular virtual balconies adding a new dimension to stateroom comfort and innovative, wholesome and awesome dining and entertainment inputs, carefully crafted for the comfort of guests. The bottom line is that the technology on display on the ship is a giant leap that will change cruise travel.

Ratna Chadha and her son Varun were also on the cruise and I could see the attention they were getting from the Royal Caribbean top brass. It was clear that their sustained efforts had taken India up the ladder in terms of business potential for the company. In fact, India ranks among the high-potential and fast-growing markets for Royal Caribbean.

The press meet over and done with, I found myself alone and decided I needed to explore the ship more.

I ascended to the top of the ship and the rewards were immediate and huge. Everywhere, as far as the eye could see, stretched the ocean, a giant swathe of silvery white with waves flaking and rippling the surface. Thanks to the giant size of the ship, we could hardly feel we were moving at all but out there, clutching the railing, some twenty stories high above the sea's surface, I got a sense of the speed of our travel. We were cutting through the water with decisive precision. Deck chairs lined both sides of the decks and were splayed out around the swimming pool. Comfortable deck chairs have a special calling for me, but I resisted the urge to settle into one of them and moved on, regardless. There was work to be done.

I had signed up for something called a Culinary Immersion Session to propagate what they call dynamic dining, whatever that is supposed to mean. Genial natured that I am, I had opted in and realized it was one of the best decisions I made on the cruise.

Dynamic dining incorporates a special dining experience that creates a new level of hospitality. The restaurants provide personalized service. Guests get something special with more a la carte dining, there's attention to the minutest detail, technology is used to enhance guests' experiences and also to help the crew provide more personalized service. The waiters take guests' meal orders but stay in the restaurant itself, using their electronic note pads to inform the chefs of what is required. It's all a bit unconventional, but effective enough. And from the guests' point of view, it is something that is noticed, relished and appreciated.

Escorted by the company's Vice President Cuisine, I did the rounds of the ship's eateries – there are 18 restaurants and 7 bars – and got a taste of the incredible dining experience on offer. The first stop on our gastronomy jaunt was Chic, which lives up to its name. Huge, classy and trendy, Chic means chic. We moved on to the classic The Grande where we'd dined the previous night. Next in line was Silk, a Chinese restaurant that offers a more social atmosphere. Then it was the turn of American Icon Grill, which provides a casual American experience.

There's still more. Jamie's Italian offers authentic Italian food. Our stop at Vintages, the wine bar, lingers in my memories – thanks mainly to the five hundred odd wines served within its haloed precincts. Michaels Genuine Pub is exactly what pubs are. Wonderland is something special – imaginative food, a lovely decor and special textures and flavours make this a rather special eatery indeed. Izumi is a typical Japanese restaurant renowned for its sushi. Chops Grilleis the signature steakhouse of Royal Caribbean. And then there is the Bionic Barwhere robots create your cocktails, a method aptly called maker-shaker.

For good measure, we also visited the Galley – the heart of the ship – where the dishes are prepared. Name the cuisine, it is there and they work to ensure it is of the highest quality.

I could have done this forever, but once again, duty called. There was more work to be done. It was show time again and in less than 24 hours I found myself back in the technological wonderland that is Two70. It was a superb performance of Mama Mia, the mood generated electric and Two70 took care of the rest.

Then came the bit I like the least and which for me, at least, always seems to come far too soon – the farewell dinner. Lonely wolf that I am, the word "farewell" never goes down well with me. But I can't say the same for the dinner. That not only went down well, but almost ruined me by raising my ever-soaring expectations. Chic isn't just a fine dining restaurant, it is a giant turf of culinary seduction. Try this for appetizers – new style Caesar salad, grilled Catalan shrimp, baby lettuce salad and pastrami

– cured salmon. The entrees list included potato crusted Iceland cod, grilled lamb T-bone, slow cooked vegetable cassoulet, baked salmon strudel and pan roasted Australian barramundi. The dessert comprised carrot cake trifle, dark chocolate torte, plum crepe mille-feuille and yogurt panna cotta.

At the risk of sounding outlandish and being totally misunderstood, I must admit that they had to literally drag me away at midnight. Which isn't that bad really, considering that they had to literally drag me off the ship the next morning.

That's my problem. I just can't tear myself away from hard work. Honestly!

28

The Blessings Seeker

"Be sweet and humble in your dealings with others. Do not allow pride to enter your heart. Sweet humility is the essence of all virtues. It never fails to win."

This was the message of Guru Harkrishan Sahib Ji, the eighth Sikh Guru, who was the second and younger son of the Seventh Guru, Guru Har Rai Sahib Ji.

Born on 7 July 1656, the child-Guru succeeded the throne in 1661 at the age of five. His short life-span lasted a mere eight years and he died on 30 March 1664. But his impact on humanity was momentous and far-reaching.

Commemorating the Guru's visit to Delhi in 1664, is the sacred Gurdwara Bangla Sahib, among the holiest of Sikh shrines and a place where humanity comes with reverence.

From dawn to dusk devotees from all religions and walks of life come here for to pay homage to the Guru. They come with their beliefs and convictions, eager to seek blessings. It is widely acknowledged that all devotees who come here get divine blessings. I firmly believe that no one leaves here empty-handed when it comes to blessings.

I try to appreciate my extreme good fortune of living in the same city as this most holy shrine, which has enabled me to come here and pay homage as often as I possibly can.

I also sometimes wonder how many more times I'll be privileged enough to do so in the future. That's how important this is for me. On several occasions, the Gurdwara has been my last source of hope, my last refuge, my saviour.

Nestled in what is now the heart of New Delhi, Gurdwara Bangla Sahib was originally a bungalow belonging to Raja Jai Singh of Amber and was known as Jaisinghpura Palace. On being invited, the Guru agreed to stay with Jai Singh during his visit to Delhi.

Because of the Guru's young age, the Raja's wife wanted to test his spiritual powers. Disguising herself as a maid servant, she sat herself down among the lady attendants. However, the Guru instantly identified her and sat on her lap, proclaiming, "This is the Rani," thereby convincing her of the great spiritual powers of Guru Nanak Dev Ji, the founder of Sikhism and the first Sikh Guru and his true disciples.

Smallpox and cholera epidemics broke out in Delhi at that time, causing great loss of life. Seeing this calamity, the Guru, out of love and compassion for the suffering, took upon himself the task of curing them. He poured charanamrit (holy water) into a chaubacha (well) and all those who took the sanctified water from the chaubacha were cured. As word spread of the Guru's great healing powers, the number of disease-stricken patients swelled and the Guru attended to them all.

Tragically, while he saved so many, the Guru himself contracted the illness and it proved to be fatal. He succumbed to the illness and died on 30 March 1664. The Guru was thereafter remembered as Bala Pir and Bala Guru in recognition of his noble deeds and great sacrifice.

A small tank was later constructed by Raja Jai Singh over the well and its amrit (holy water) is revered as being sacred and endowed with healing properties.

A small gurdwara was first built at the site by the Sikh General, Sardar Bhagel Singh in 1783, who supervised the construction of nine Sikh shrines in Delhi in the same year. In time, the gurdwara became bigger in terms of its physical proportions.

Today, Bangla Sahib is resplendent with its marble facade, magnificent dome, large sarovar (water tank), nishan sahib (flagpole), landscaped gardens and ached marble gates. And it is resplendent in its cleanliness, which is a hallmark of all gurdwaras around the world.

The building's interior is equally beautiful. The vast hall is ornate but not opulent. The Guru Granth Sahib (holy book of the Sikhs) is placed on a gold-plated palanquin that rests on a marble platform. The ceiling directly above this spot is also entirely gold-plated, as are the large pillars that flank it. A giant, four-piece chandelier hangs from the ceiling just in front of the Guru Granth Sahib. The ceiling on the two sides of the hall is also ornate, sporting large, elegant chandeliers. The gurdwara complex includes the shrine itself, a kitchen and langar hall, a tourist information centre and Baba Baghel Singh Museum.

Devotees from all castes, sects and religions visit the gurdwara, pay their respects before the holy Guru Granth Sahib, listen to the kirtan and drink the amrit from the curative chaubacha.

As with all Sikh gurdwaras, the concept of langar (free food) is practised with great grace and humility and all people, regardless of race or religion, may eat in the gurdwara langar hall during the day and night, throughout the year.

Many people, especially foreigners, find it hard to believe that Sikh gurdwaras provide free food every day to everyone, irrespective of their caste, creed or nationality. But that is exactly what they do, all over India and indeed, all over the world. Providing free food as langar stems from the will of Guru Nanak Dev Ji. It is the Sikh way.

As I mentioned, I try to bring myself here as often as I can. When the chips are down, I come here with my personal issues and problems, and I dare say, I have reaped rich benefits. I have managed to weather many a storm simply by praying here, at this most holy, exalted shrine. I also try to do a little seva (service) whenever I can. Sewa at gurdwaras can include everything from cleaning the premises, to attending to the devotees' footwear, to helping out in the kitchen or serving langar. The Gurus themselves started and partook in the concept of sewa. This is also the Sikh way.

In a prayer written by Guru Gobind Singh Sahib Ji in the Dasam Granth (Sikh holy book), Sikhs recite the following verse every day:

"Meditate then on revered Harkrishan,

On seeing whom, all suffering vanishes."

While this noble saying is heard and followed the world over by Sikhs, the centre of it all is Gurdwara Bangla Sahib.